TUGS BOOMS & BARGES

The Story of the Tugs and Crews In British Columbia and Puget Sound

R. SHERET

WESTERN ISLES

Canadian Cataloguing in Publication Data

Sheret, R.E. (Robin Edward), 1932-
  Tugs, booms & barges

Includes bibliographical references and index.
ISBN O-921107-08-0

1. Tugboats--British Columbia--History. 2 Tugboats--Washington (State)--Puget Sound--History. 3. Coastwise shipping--British Columbia--History. 4. Coastwise shipping--Washington (State)--Puget Sound--History. I. Title.
VM464.S54 1999   387.2'32'09711   C99-910142-0

Front cover
Seaspan Valiant running light off Galiano Island.
Photo by R. Sheret

WESTERN ISLES

Western Isles Cruise and Dive Co. Ltd.
2962 Leigh Rd.,
Victoria B.C. V9B 4G3
Canada

First Edition 1999

Printed in Canada

CONTENTS

Contents

INTRODUCTION

The tugs have made a major contribution to the economy of the coast of British Columbia, Alaska and in Puget Sound. The life on a work boat trying to compete in a difficult environment is far different from that of a pleasure boat. We hope this will help people understand the industry and the people that work in it from the managers to the deck hands.

The main problem we had in putting this book together was what to leave out. The industry has had such a history in Puget Sound and British Columbia that it would fill many books. We tried to convey a small part of what it is like to work on a tug and the many types of towing operations. The reader will be able to follow the development of the coastal tug from the early steam tugs to the modern tractor tug. The methods of navigation used in the period are also discussed.

There are many types of towing operations on the coast. Unlike many other parts of the world tug and tow operations handle most coastal cargos in the area. The forest industry requires huge amounts of wood to keep the mills operating. Most of this material is brought in by tugs. In remote areas supplies often arrive by barge.

Notes

As the book is designed for readers that are not part of the industry we have tried to avoid getting too technical. The editors have reduced the amount of nautical terms in order to reduce confusion. Contrary to popular beliefs the terms used in the industry are not bad english. They have come down from many years of seafaring.

Throughout the book we have tried to compare the past with the present. This we hope will give the reader some idea of the development that has taken place in the industry.

Photos

Unless otherwise noted all photographs and illustrations are by Robin Sheret. They are copyright © by R. Sheret and Western Isles Cruise and Dive Co. Ltd.

We have tried to use the name of the vessel and company at the time the photograph was taken when possible.

Credits

Project editor J. Green, Copy Editor C. Rutherford. Design & typesetting by Western Isles, printing, binding and colour scan by Friesen Printers. Design and layout produced on Power Macintosh computers using Quark 3.3, technical illustrations on Canvas 3.5.

Thanks to the many people that assisted us with this project.

In particular:

Captain J. Dean, Captain M. Freeman -Fremont Tugboat Company, Debbie Tardiff- Seaspan International.

1
TUGS & MACHINERY

The Lorne, built 1889 in Victoria by Robert Dunsmuir for towing sailing ships to Nanaimo and Union bay and back to Juan de Fuca Strait. Registered length 151 ft. (46 m.) GT 288 with a 114 nhp. steam engine. She was a coal burner.
B.C. Archives

Burrard Chief was owned by Island Tug and Barge at this time. Built in Vancouver in 1919. Reg. length 67 ft.(20 m.) 27 nhp. She was typical of a lot of Canadian and American tugs of the era.
B.C. Archives

Spray, built in Vancouver in 1907 for Victoria Tug Co. reg. length 81 ft. (25 m.) 22.5 nhp. She towed coal from Nanaimo and Union Bay. She towed some of the sailing ships. She was a coal burner at this time. Later she was an oil burner and had a shorter stack with a v on it. She had a raised after deck. Good sea boat.
B.C. Archives

INTRODUCTION

Joining a crew boarding a tug at night, you are soon aware that you are entering a world unknown to most shore dwellers. The boat seems very cold, dark and lifeless. As each man arrives with his gear, the boat starts to come alive. The coffee pot is put on as soon as there is light in the galley and heat on the stove. On a modern diesel vessel this will require the engineer to start an auxiliary. On the old steam tugs a coal-oil lamp was lit followed by the coal-burning galley stove. The engineers were generally the first ones on board to get steam up and light the galley stove.

Each man heads for his quarters to stow his gear and change into his work clothes. Before electricity, lamps had to be lit in all areas. The seamen, mate, cook and off-watch engineers grab a coffee. The captain comes aboard with the orders. If there is a new deck hand, he will be told what watch he is on. The mate starts to get the crew organized, getting grub (food) and deck stores aboard. Many boxes of grub are brought down the dock to be loaded on the vessel. As the boxes arrive on board, the cook starts stowing all the provisions.

When everything including deck stores is aboard, the mate and the on-watch seaman will get the towing gear ready for the first job. Meanwhile, the skipper will get things organized in the wheelhouse.

If not needed to get away with the tow, the off-watch people head below to make their bunks and try to get some sleep. The wheelhouse lights are shut off, the lines are let go and the boat slowly leaves her berth. As soon as the deck is secure the deck lights go out and the boat, now a living thing, is on her way to her first job.

The type of coast found from Puget Sound to Juneau, Alaska, consisting of many islands, shoals, strong tidal currents, long stretches of protected waters and long inlets, made it difficult to operate sailing ships. The need to tow the windjammers, along with the logging industries' requisites to have logs moved to the mills, were the reasons the British Columbia and Puget Sound towboat industries started to develop in the middle of the 19th century. The type of coast, the forest industry, the need to move supples and products to the coastal areas of Alaska are reasons why it is still an economically viable business. The fact that it is an ice-free coast makes this type of transportation viable year round. It was, and still is, a business that uses relatively small craft with small crews to move a large quantity of product.

There have been many changes on the coast since the first tug towed sailing ships and a few small log booms. Great industries, that would not have been dreamed of at first, later located on the coast and up the rivers. They all needed reliable transportation and they found it in the towboat fleets.

A different type of steam tug and later diesel tug developed in the lakes and some rivers. Farther south below the Columbia River, coastal tugs were used more for harbour or long-haul barge work.

Tugs were one of the reasons a lot of effort went into developing steam power at sea. An Englishman, with the appropriate name of Hull, in 1736 patented a machine for towing vessels out of or into any harbour, port or river against any wind or in a calm (a tug). Unfortunately, his experiments in 1737 failed. A beam engine was patented in the 1770s but it was not till 1803 that Fulton actually got the first steamboat to work commercially.

What was eventually to become the first tug on the west coast of North America was built in England, in 1835. The Beaver, equipped with two 35 horsepower sidelever engines, arrived in 1836.

There were a number of paddlewheel tugs used in the early days. As the engines improved in power and reliability, the usefulness of tugs for moving cargo increased. When triple expansion engines were introduced larger tugs were built. The diesel engine brought yet more power in a smaller package along with smaller crews. For years the steamers worked in the same areas as the newer diesels. Due to different government regulations, the steam tugs lasted longer in Canada than in the United States.

At first, tugs were too underpowered to compete with coastal freighters for cargos where speed of delivery was important. This slowly changed as smaller and more powerful engines were developed. A big advantage tugs have over coastal freighters is they often do not have to wait while cargo is loaded or discharged. By working with a variety of barges they can move a large assortment of cargos with the same tug and crew.

The ideal situation is one tow loading, one tow in route and one tow unloading. This only happens with certain types of operations such as chip and hog fuel scows. Tugs can pick up and drop off parts of their tow in several ports while on one trip (voyage). Smaller boats can take a

The Sea Lion, 114 ft. (35 m.) 211.33 GT. Built in 1905, Vancouver.
She was originally built for log towing. She was noted for her unusual whistle that could play a tune when entering First Narrows. She was later converted to diesel (800 hp). She was on a steady run to Prince Rupert with a chemical barge. After her days as a tug were over, she became a research vessel.
Photographer unknown.

Right: The front of the Master's housework. The ladder from the fore deck to the boat deck was typical of most steam tugs. In bad weather it was hard to stay dry on the way to the wheelhouse. The wheelhouses on these vessels are quite small.
The Master is preserved by the SS Master Society in Vancouver, B.C.

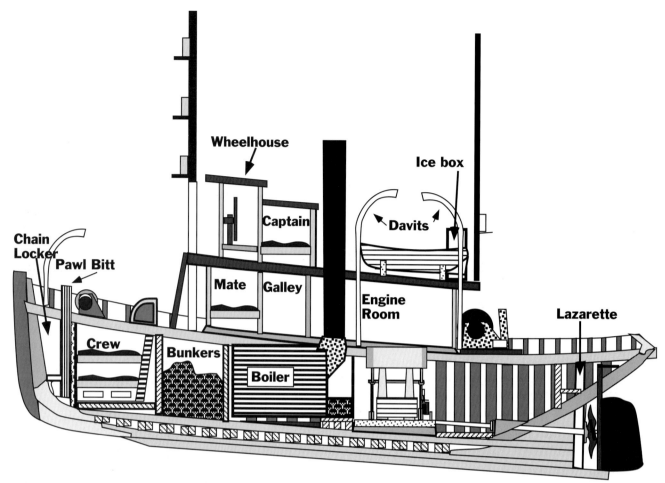

The layout of a typical steam tug. There were many variations on the basic design. American and Canadian steam tugs were similar but had to meet the inspection standards of the country they were registered in. These tugs towed logs and scows all over the coast.

The towing winch Katahdin. Some of the winches were not too sophisticated. The 73 ft. (22.3 m.) vessel built in 1899 was originally a steam tug before Foss converted it to diesel. She is in private ownership now.

barge off a bigger tug and deliver it to a dock that the bigger tug could not reach. To save time small boats can yard up tows for the bigger boat. Tugs can assist other types of transportation from rail to deep-sea ships. Construction companies rely on them to deliver material on time and move equipment.

This requires a highly organized shore staff and good communication. For years before radio, communication to the office was difficult. If the skipper could find a shore phone, he would contact the office for orders and give a progress report.

We see the big companies that dominate the coast today and forget that the industry started with small, one or two boat operations. Foss, one of the largest companies, started with rowboats in Tacoma, Washington. Dolmage, which became a large, independent, Canadian towboat company, was started by 19 year old Bill Dolmage. As time went on, it became harder to compete with the big outfits. One of the earliest mill and towboat companies on the sound, Pope & Talbot, now have logging, mill and towing operations on the Arrow Lakes in British Columbia.

After World War 11, the forest industry increased on the B.C. coast. Many new lumber and pulp mills were built. New tugs and barges were built to service them. In the 1960s smaller and more powerful engines came along. Small steel-hulled tugs were built to take advantage of these

PAWL BITT

ANCHOR TACKLE

STEAM ANCHOR WINCH

CREW ACCOMMODATION

The fore deck of the Master as seen from above. The anchor would normally be stowed on deck. It was lifted over the side with the aid of the anchor davit, tackle and steam winch. Bow lines were made fast on the pawl bitt. (A name left over from the days of sail). Some of the crew slept below. They would use the companionway to get on deck which could present a problem in heavy weather.

engines. The industry developed in the 1960s and 70s before leveling off. In the late 1980s and during the 90s a number of the lumber mills were permanently closed. The areas that could be logged were reduced. Pressure from environmental groups reduced the forest industry even more, especially when it was discovered there was a lot of money to be made in environmental causes. This, of course, had an adverse affect on the towboat industry.

There have been many changes in the industry over the years. Without dedicated and highly trained personnel willing to try new things, the industry would have disappeared in its infancy.

COASTAL WOODEN TUGS

The west coast, coastal tug evolved differently than did the ocean-going tugs of Europe and the east coast. The eastern tugs are used on the coast but are noticeably different than the smaller, versatile west coasters. For years many local tugs were constructed of wood.

From the start of the towing industry till the 1950s, wooden tugs made money for their owners. With the increase in the power of the engines and size of the tows, steel vessels replaced most of them. A number of these vessels were originally built for other purposes. Some started their careers as sailing vessels, fishing vessels, passen-

The Queen, built 1914 reg. length 84.7 ft. (25.8 m.). She originally had a 23 nominal hp steam engine. She towed logs for several companies including Cliff and Rivtow.

M.R. Cliff was a famous logtower on the coast. One of the Cliff Tugboat Co. fleet, though owned by Rivtow Marine when this photograph was taken.

When sail still hauled most of the lumber and coal, many steam tugs were engaged in towing them.

ger boats or naval vessels. In the early days, most tugs served a dual roll as tug and passenger vessels.

Some of the original tugs were paddlewheelers such as the Beaver (Can.), the Goliath (U.S.), the Favorite (U.S.) and the Alexander (Canadian). Paddlewheelers were used on the rivers and lakes for many years. The first tug built in B.C. was the sidewheeler, Isabel, in 1866. She did not look much like a tug and had housework running right aft in order to carry passengers. She also had the distinction of losing the sailing ship, Fanny, in 1868. The Fanny wound up on Discovery Island where divers still look at her bones. There were a number of paddlewheel boats operating in Puget Sound. The last Canadian sidewheeler was the Alexander, built in 1873.

While not technically a tug, the American sidewheeler, Del Norte, made many tows to Alaska. She sank near Porlier Pass, B.C. in 1868. She was also the first major ocean-going vessel (192 ft. 601 tons) built in San Francisco.

The first steam tug built in Vancouver was the 70 ft.(21m.), 20 nominal horsepower, Maggie, in 1873; another vessel with the housework running all the way aft. This must have made steering a tow next to impossible as a tug on a short towline can only turn if it is made fast well forward of the rudder. As some of the early tugs doubled as passenger and freight boats, they put the tow bitts on top of the housework. Stability was another problem as the high location of the tow bitts would make the vessel vulnerable to capsizing if the tow got off to one side.

The first British Columbian vessels built for towing alone were the Active and Lorne in 1889. They even looked like tugs. They were not noted for their handling abilities. Towing winches were added later.

A number of early American tugs did not have wheelhouses until they started losing too many skippers. Until recent times, most towboats were not noted for their spacious wheelhouses nor often the ability to see anything aft from them. The large wheel took up most of the room in the wheelhouse. If you were lucky, there might be room for a pull down chart table. Working out a course on one of these chart tables on a rolling vessel in the middle of the night, could make a phone booth feel spacious.

At first, the steamers burnt wood. When mines opened up on Vancouver Island, coal became the fuel of choice. Wood was not a very efficient fuel. Copious amounts of wood were needed to keep a boat operating. A vessel could get held up until enough wood was cut. While this helped the local employment, it made towing a bit impractical.

There were still some coal burners around in the late 1940s and early 50s. Oil started replacing coal in the 1930s. Diesel engines started replacing steam before WW11. Due to different crewing regulations, the American boats were converted to diesel earlier than the Canadian boats. When comparing horsepower figures of the different engines, you have to be careful not to equate brake horsepower of the diesel tug with indicated horsepower of the steam tug.

The early tugs required a large crew. The wood burners needed a lot of men ashore just to keep the vessel supplied with fuel. At the turn of the century, a vessel like the 288 GT. Lorne had a 14-man crew. In the 1940s the 85 GT. coal-burning tug, Swell, had an 8-man crew. The coming of oil and diesel reduced the crews greatly.

As the boats did not handle like those of today, it was not only the engines that needed a large crew. There was no power steering or power anything else. There were no towing winches on the early tugs. The heavy hawsers were hard to handle and needed a larger deck crew. A lot of the boats did not have a telegraph and used "bells and jingles" to relay engine manoeuvres to the engineer.

Wooden tugs were built in a manner similar to a sailing vessel except for the stern. However, the construction was heavier especially around the stern and bow sections. Tugs usually had double-planking, at least down to just below the water line. This planking was usually a hard wood, known as iron wood or iron bark. They had heavy guards running from stem to stern. If the boats did not get too many bumps from scows, the wooden hulls lasted for years. The constant bumping against barges took its toll on the sterns and bulwarks of the wooden scow boats.

The older wooden tugs were long and narrow by today's standard. They were usually very good seaboats. The stern of any well-designed tug is rounded so the towline will not hang up when the vessel is turning. It must be fairly full (wider) to give stability when towing. The rudder on a tug should be bigger than a vessel of similar size. The rudder should not protrude past the stern guard or it could be damaged when backing up to a boom or scow. These tugs had lots of draught and swung a big propeller. The bow should not have much rake so it can be used to push on barges, ships, or booms. Logtowers will have metal teeth (log teeth) on the bow around the waterline for gripping the logs when pushing. The teeth are also good for accidentally punching holes in scows if the skipper is not careful.

Boats engaged in ship or barge work will have big fenders on the bow and sides. For years these were made of rope, but fenders made of rubber eventually replaced them.

Island Monarch - Island Tug. 1800 opposed piston Fairbanks Morse. Reg. length 157.6 ft. (48 m.). Originally a large WWII ATR class steam tug later converted to diesel. These tugs were about as big as they could build out of wood.

Le Beau, Vancouver Tug in Victoria.

The Island Ranger. Reg. length 68.2 ft. (21 m.) 500 hp. This was a ST class tug built for the U.S. military. After repowering she was known as a hot rod, towing 2 loads to Duncan Bay. After the new steel tugs arrived in the 1960s along with bigger chippers, she was considered totally under powered. Up to the 1960s, many tugs had only 200 to 400 hp.

Just a bit late going astern Cap't?

Wooden Miki-type tug. The U.S. WWII wooden tugs saw service all over the world. Some of them were used in the Vietnam War. They were around 118 feet (36 m.) long. The single screw vessels were called Mikis. The twin screw ones were known as Miki-Miki. Originally slow speed diesels around 1,270 hp.

The Sirmack, owned by Victoria Tug before becoming part of the Island Tug fleet. These vessels, TP class tugs, built for the U.S. Army. Reg. length 92 feet (28 m.) with a 400 hp. Fairbanks Morse slow speed diesel.

Seaspan Challenger, formerly Is. Challenger. 765 hp. A lot of these TP class vessels were repowered with smaller and more powerful engines. The housework was also changed to some degree.

Scow boats would also have a heavy fender on the stern. This fender served the purposes of protecting the stern of the tug, the bow of the scow and kept the stern from sliding on the barge when the tug was backing up on it.

The housework was kept well in from the sides of the hull so it would less likely be damaged when working alongside ships and large barges. The housework could not extend too far aft or it would interfere with the towline. There had to be space on the fore deck for the crew to handle lines and room for heavy bollards and anchor winches. This did not leave too much room for the crew's quarters. A lot of logtowers had a low wheelhouse while most scow boats were designed with a high wheelhouse. The skipper's cabin was usually just behind the wheelhouse so the mate could call him quickly if needed.

Lifeboats were stowed on the upper or boat deck. The old, iron davits ran from the main deck near the bulwarks to above the boat deck. They were always getting bent by the scows. They could hang up on any protrusion when the skipper was trying to slide the boat up the side of a barge. The lifeboats dried out in the heat and had a tendency to sink when launched. If you left them in the water long enough, the wood would swell and make them tight again.

Originally, tugs were used for towing sailing ships and logs. In order to tow the ships in Juan de Fuca Strait, the tugs had to be pretty good seaboats. As time went on, the fleet started to specialize. Some companies worked in the coastal log trade only. Tugs built for this purpose usually had less freeboard to facilitate the crews working on the low, flat booms. This was not because owners worried about the crews working too hard, but rather about the time lost getting off and on the boat with heavy log gear.

Some companies went into barge work exclusively. The tugs built for this work had more freeboard, could take more weather and had heavier fenders. Small river boats were developed for working the rivers. These were very manoeuvrable, shallower-draft vessels. Open-water barge and salvage work developed another type of large, powerful ship.

The propellers were changed for the type of work the vessel did. Logtowers had a "log wheel" for getting the maximum power while towing heavy log booms. When towing the faster moving barges they were not too efficient. By the same token, scow boats with a lot of pitch in their wheels, had problems with their diesel engines heating up when towing logs. Companies that were engaged in general towing used a compromise wheel.

The engines and boilers were big and took up a part of the housework. The galley/mess was in the housework as was the chief's and possibly the mate's room. The second engineer could have a room on deck too. Most boats had a wheelhouse on the boat deck with the skipper's cabin right behind it.

On most boats the seamen, firemen and cooks slept down below in the fo'c'sel. Despite the crew's best efforts, this could become a damp, smelly place. Coal dust seeped into it more readily than the rest of the boat. Some of the larger tugs had quarters on deck for the entire crew.

Most boats did not have any inside passages. You had to climb a ladder on the front of the housework to get to the wheelhouse.

Wire towlines were eventually used in most places on the west coast due to the deeper water, unlike Europe or the east coast where rope hawsers were the norm. This made towing winches practical. It also kept the crew size down as one man could shorten up or pay out line. Eventually, all but the smallest harbour tugs had a steam-driven towing winch. When steam was replaced by diesel the winches were driven by electricity or hydraulics.

There usually was an anchor winch located on the fore deck. With the stock anchor normally found on these boats, the anchor had to be rigged on deck and heaved over the side with the aid of an anchor davit and a tackle. The stock anchor stowed inboard, did not hang up on scows like the stockless anchor stowed in a hawse pipe.

As a tug frequently handles its tow with deck lines, she would use much heavier lines than a vessel of similar size engaged in another trade. The deck was usually wide and there were very heavy bitts and cleats on deck to take the heavy lines. There was often a heavy, wooden bitt or post, called a pawl bitt, near the bow. This was used for securing bow lines when handling a barge alongside. There would be spring line cleats located forward on each side of the vessel. Approximately where the housework ended back aft, there would be stern line cleats. Large steel bollards could replace cleats on some vessels.

Over the long life of one of these wooden tugs it may have a number of owners, names and areas of operation. The Arthur Foss was an example of this. She was built in Portland as the steam tug, Wallowa, in 1889 for towing ships across the Columbia River bar. In 1898, she came to Seattle to tow gold rush supplies to Skagway for the Pacific Clipper Line. In 1900, she was owned by Puget Sound Sawmills of Bellingham. She then went to Merril & Ring Lumber Company.

Foss Launch and Tug Co. bought her in 1934. In 1937, she had a fire on board but was rebuilt. The navy took her over during the War. After the War she was again

Bell & Jingle Code to Engineer

STOP TO FULL AHEAD:		
STOP TO SLOW	———	JINGLE, BELL
STOP TO HALF	———	BELL
SLOW TO HALF	———	JINGLE,BELL
HALF TO FULL	———-	JINGLE
FULL AWAY	———-	SEVERAL JINGLES
FULL AHEAD TO STOP:		
FULL TO HALF	———-	BELL
FULL TO STOP	———-	TWO BELLS
HALF TO STOP	———-	BELL
HALF TO SLOW	———-	BELL,JINGLE,BELL
SLOW TO STOP	———-	BELL
STOP TO FULL ASTERN:		
STOP TO SLOW ASTERN	—	JINGLE,TWO BELLS
STOP TO HALF ASTERN	—-	TWO BELLS
STOP TO FULL ASTERN	—-	TWO BELLS,JINGLE
HALF TO FULL ASTERN	—	JINGLE
FULL ASTERN TO STOP:		ONE BELL
(stops all astern movements).		

Dauntless, a small logtower. There were many boats that just towed logs and the occasional scow.

Island Trooper, assisting a ship. Wooden harbour tugs became too small as the ships got bigger. Boats such as these did not have towing winches.

Hurry up and take this barge. Did you bring a paper?

The Sea Wave, alongside a tow in Port Renfrew. A lot of vessels built for log towing had a low wheelhouse. This made it hard to see what you were doing when landing a scow. Reg. length 75.2 feet (23m.) 600 hp.

Small wooden logtower.

put to work in the sound until she was laid up in 1968, seventy-nine years after she was built.

In 1912, the steam tug, Swell, was built for Victoria Tug. She was re-powered in the 1950s and is still operating today. Many tugs did not have that long a life.

In addition to tugs built for the job, many other vessels were adapted to meet the requirements of the industry. During WW11 many wooden tugs were built for the military. After the War, these wound up in civilian use on both sides of the border. These boats were often re-engined. They operated for years towing material around the coast.

STEEL TUGS

Iron and steel tugs have been used in the industry for years. Most of them were either large tugs built for off-shore operations or vessels such as trawlers, converted from some other trade to tugs. It was not until the late 50s that modern steel tugs were built to replace the many wooden tugs in the fleet.

Steel tugs will, all being equal, take more weather and contact with barges than wooden boats. They will stand up to the rigors of handling big, steel barges. Larger horsepower engines can be installed without creating stress problems. They suffer from being damper as metal "sweats" if not heated, or insulated and vented properly. This can make living quarters uncomfortable. This became more evident when diesels were installed. If they run into difficulties they can sink in minutes.

The older tugs were usually built of riveted iron or steel plates. They had a long life and often went through several engines. At first, they were all steamers but became good candidates for diesel conversion.

Not all the older steel and iron tugs started their life as a tug, and like their wooden counterparts, had a varied life. Some came to British Columbia as fishing vessels and ended up as tugs. The Island Commander, Island Warrior, A.G. Garrish and the Newington were some of the fishing vessels that became tugs.

The Newington, built in Hull, U.K. in 1899, fished halibut in B.C. before becoming a R.C.N. vessel in WW1. She remained a government vessel as a lighthouse tender after the War. Pacific Coyle purchased her for ocean towing in 1937. Unlike most of the others, she remained a steamer.

The large ones that had been built for off-shore work were small ships with the latest navigation equipment for the time. They had long after decks. This gave problems handling towlines so strongbacks, sometimes called tow spans, or Dutch tow bars, were installed. These prevented the heavy towline from lying on deck. As the towing gear on large tugs is very heavy, capstans are used with a light line to move it around the deck.

American-designed tugs usually had the housework running further aft than did the European-designed vessels. This made them less manoeuvrable on the towline because the tow bitts or winch was further aft. As the housework was over top of the engines this gave them more room for machinery. Most of the European-designed large tugs unlike most earlier American tugs, had a high fo'c'sel extending aft to the engine room. These tugs were deep

Nitinat Chief, near Becher Bay. Originally built for logs she towed scows and logs.

draft and heavy enabling them to keep a steady course and pull in heavy seas.

In addition to open-water towing, these large tugs were used for salvage work. Some of them such as the Salvage Queen, the Salvage King and the Sudburys were fitted out with extra pumps and salvage gear. There were many successful operations done with these vessels. The boats were big enough to stow all this equipment and often had small machine shops and even decompression chambers for divers. At one time, some of these large tugs were used for towing rail barges on the inside passage. Later, this job was taken over by much smaller tugs.

The living quarters on these tugs were often better than those of their smaller relations. The crews were much larger than the smaller boats. The salvage tugs often carried a diver. The seamen and firemen usually slept in a fo'c'sel. These were generally located up forward just aft of the chain locker. Bunks were situated on each side of the fo'c'sel and were two high. The bunk would be rigged with a curtain for privacy. The officers had their own room though a couple of junior officers might have to share. The officers would have their own mess and heads. There was more room to move around and relax than on a smaller tug. Of course, they were out in bad weather for longer periods as well. Getting tossed out of the bunk by the violent action of the boat was not uncommon.

As newer diesel and electrical equipment was developed crews were reduced even more. The horsepower and manoeuvrability also increased.

There were a lot of smaller steel tugs on the coast as well. Steel tugs such as the U.S. registered, Standard #3, were built for harbour and coastal work. While some were built for towing on the coast more of them were originally built for other reasons. The old Island Mariner was an example of this. She was originally the Madge, a quarantine

Above: The Gillking. When she towed cement scows for Gilly Brothers she was considered a powerhouse with 600 hp. She now tows logs for Pacific Towing.
Below: The Fraser Crown. They were built as U.S. Army harbour tugs. They had some stability problems so the size of the housework was reduced. A similar type boat sank off Oak Bay with only one survivor.

The Mercer Straits, 2,200 hp. 95 ft. (29 m.). She is one of the newer style steel tugs that can handle many types of jobs around the coast.

I see the deck department finally got an E.T.A. that was right on.

vessel. The Wedell Foss also started her career as a quarantine vessel. Some tugs, such as the Kenai, started their careers as passenger ships.

During WW11 a vast number of tugs were constructed. The hull design usually followed traditional tug lines. When these vessels became war surplus at the end of hostilities, a number of them were put to use on the coast.

The big change in tugs came in the 1960s as the wooden tugs were being phased out. A more powerful engine could be put in a small hull. Canadian towboat companies took full advantage of this. Under the regulations of the day, small steel tugs of around 40 to 65 feet(12-20m.) were built without much thought to safety or living conditions. Often the living quarters were cramped, damp holes without any method of escape in an emergency. There was no way of preventing down flooding if the vessel was heeled over. A number of these vessels were lost as were their crews.

Other companies, such as Island Tug and Vancouver Tug, had a different approach to tug construction. They took advantage of modern hull design from naval architects such as Robert Allan. Kort Nozzles were introduced along with a lot of power and other modern equipment. The Kort Nozzles were either fixed with rudders or the steering type that moved on a heavy shaft to steer the vessel. The propeller turned inside the nozzle to give the extra thrust. The tugs were larger running around 70 to 100 feet(21-30m.). Most of these boats are working today.

Unlike traditional tugs, the hulls were designed to supply a clean flow of water to the nozzle or nozzles. They often had hard chines which made construction cheaper. They were very stable, which along with the hull design, made them safe but frequently a bit quick in a sea. Some of them could roll 30 degrees without too much trouble.

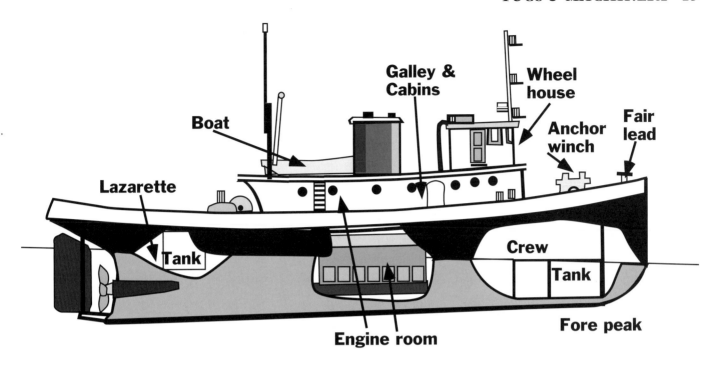

V2ME-A1 Harbour tug. An earlier type of American steel tug. These type were U.S.N. yard tugs.

Unfortunately, in order to keep the housework small most of the crew slept below the waterline. Due to the higher speed engines and the auxiliaries required to meet the electrical requirements, most of these vessels were very noisy. The galleys on these vessels were big and comfortable. You could go anywhere in the vessel without having to go on deck which reduced the chance of getting washed overboard in bad weather.

In 1970, The Canadian Merchant Service Guild went on strike to improve the safety conditions on the Canadian tugs. As with all labour disputes, there were arguments from both sides. The Government did a study and brought in many new regulations. Watertight hatches (that worked) had to be installed along with a lot of other measures to stop down flooding. Living conditions, hours of work and noise levels were also addressed. Some of the small steel boats wound up working only as day boats after some upgrading.

Another feature was the requirement of a quick release for the towing winch at all steering stations. Before this, there was no way of releasing the winch unless you could get someone back to the brake. A large barge or ship could roll over a tug before anyone could let the brake go. These, and other safety features, made the tugs far more useful.

As the accommodation had to be above the waterline, a lot of the newer tugs were built with high bows. These vessels looked a bit ugly at first, but proved to work well. Noise reduction was introduced on these newer vessels as well.

The next big development in tug design was the tractor and reverse-tractor tugs. They were originally designed for ship docking but more of them are being used for general towing.

Above: Sandra Foss, entering Bellingham. A twin screw tug. She had been assisting a tanker.
Below: Joseph T., Astoria, Oregon, after assisting another tug.

Foss assist tug in Astoria.

The Pacific Crest returning to base in Port Alberni. 52 ft. (16 m.) 900 hp. Owned by Pacific Towing Services Ltd. Below: The J.S. Dol Hemos, Corp. of Engineer boat Juneau, Alaska. There are many tugs that work in Alaska. Some Alaskan companies tow to Seattle while others work locally.

They can pull off the bow as well as the stern. In fact, most of them have a winch on the bow as well as on the stern. They do not have the problem of getting in irons (getting rolled over if a strain comes on the towline from the side) as a conventional tug would. This has always been a problem for tugs handling ships, and at times, large barges.

Pusher tugs have been used on the American east coast for years. There are now some on the west coast as well. These tugs fit into a notch in the barge so they are one unit. They can work in some fairly big seas. Some ordinary barges have been pushed for years but there are limits as to how much swell they can take.

We can be sure that there will be advances in the design of the tugs and their equipment in the future. If trends continue as they have, the tugs will become more powerful as tows get bigger.

THE COMPANIES

Most of the early tugs were owned by the mills, mines, or fishing companies that used them. A lot of the big forest companies maintained their own fleet of tugs up to recent times. Today, the bulk of the work is done by general towing companies, although there are still a number of smaller operators in business.

It would be impossible to name all the tugboat companies that have worked in the area. A number of them were started in the late 19th and early 20th centuries. They often combined to become the large companies we now know. As an example of this, Island Tug started by buying some small companies. It later purchased Victoria Tug and Young and Gore. It amalgamated with Vancouver Tug to become Seaspan. Seaspan in turn purchased Gulf of Georgia Towing, along with some boats and crews from other companies. Seaspan is now part of the Washington Marine Group comprised of a number of older companies.

The earlier large companies were often owned by families, such as Foss and Elworthy of Island Tug. Eventually, corporations bought them out. The names of the older companies have often been used again with completely different owners.

The crews frequently worked for a number of operators in their careers. The tugs often had several names and have also been bought, sold, repowered and rebuilt. This makes it difficult to keep track of the ships and the crews.

Edith Love Joy, a 75 ft. (23 m.) 1,125 hp. tug owned by Puget Sound Freight Limited. She towed paper barges. In most ports the crew loaded and unloaded the barges.

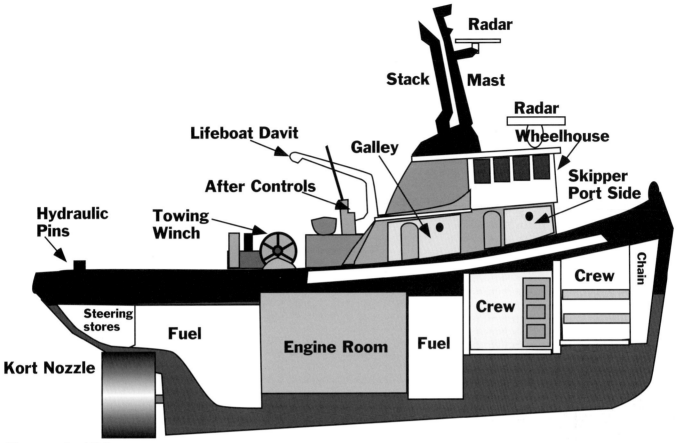

Radar

Stack **Mast**

Radar

Wheelhouse

Lifeboat Davit

Galley

Skipper Port Side

After Controls

Hydraulic Pins

Towing Winch

Crew **Chain**

Crew

Steering stores

Fuel

Engine Room **Fuel**

Kort Nozzle

Diagram of a 1970s type tug.

The Kingcome, 92 ft (28 m.). 1,125 hp. logtower owned by Kingcome Navigation Ltd. Now part of the Washington Marine Group. These vessels, unlike the small hot rods of the 60s, are comfortable boats.

The Navigator, a 9,000 Invader class tug with 7,200 hp. on its way to Alaska. These vessels are capable of working anywhere in the world. They tow a lot of equipment and supplies to the North Slope. Owned by Crowley Marine Services (Red Stack). These tugs when loaded down with fuel do not have much freeboard. Before going out into open water everything is "tied down" on the main deck which will be awash most of the time.

Richard Foss, one of the tugs escorting a ship out of Port Angeles. They had just got her away from the dock.

Cap! They changed the weather forecast from light winds to a gale warning.

The Seaspan Star, running light in a bit of a chop. This 65 ft. (20 m.) 765 hp. tug was built in the 60s for Vancouver Tug. Used for general towing.

Swiftsure 3, logtower owned by Swiftsure Towing.

Storm Force, 68 ft. (21 m.) 1,450 hp. scow boat owned by Shields Towing.

The after deck of the Seaspan Chief. As with most coastal tugs she has a single drum towing winch. The chains stowed along the bulwarks are used for towing scows in open water. Just forward of the life boat there is a control center. In addition to steering and engine controls, the master can operate the towing winch and the hydraulic pins on the stern. These pins keep the towline over the stern so it will not get in the wheel when she is yarding. It also keeps the towline over the stern when she has a long line out. If the line were to jump the pins, it could get caught under the stern or pull the boat over (girding). The towline is tied down in open water so this will not happen. On some of the newer tugs the tie-down equipment can be operated from the after station.

There are three pins. The wide ones are used when she is heaving the bridles aboard or paying them out. This will let the shackle through. The narrow pins are used when the tug is underway. This reduces the amount of wear on the towline. When towing in open water a steel pad is bolted to the towline to reduce wear.

The narrow pins are also used to reduce the amount of towline travel when the crew is shackling or knocking off the towline links.

Left: Margaret Foss, 2,200 hp. in the locks. She has twin drums so she can put a barge on each towline. She is also rigged to make up to a ship for docking.

Swiftsure X. Owned by Swiftsure Towing. Older type of large tug built for off-shore towing.

Hecket Crown - Crown Zellerbach. The high bow is carried well back on this ocean-going tug.

LOST TUGS

While many tugs had a long and varied career others met a sudden end. There were a number of reasons for the loss of these vessels including: weather, tow problems, navigational errors and unseaworthy boats. A lot of the boats were lost for unknown reasons often with their crews. Some of the boats are listed below:

Andrew Foss 1951 collision	Men lost 1
Arthur B 1910 weather	Men lost 6
B & M 1928 fire explosion	Men lost 1
Baer 1951	
Bahada 1926 ? possible boiler	Whole crew
Bentinck 1941 hit rock	Men lost 3
C.P. York 1953 hit reef	Men lost 5
Chelan 1954 ?	Whole crew
Farquhar 1930 ? weather	Men lost 6
Fearless 1899 ?	Men lost 7
George McGregor 1949 ? weather	Men lost 6
Gulf Master 1967 ?	Men lost 5
Henry Foss 1959 hit rock	Men lost 6
Leslie T 1932 weather	Men lost 1
Mainland Prince 1966 ?	Men lost 1
Marlyn 1951 weather	Men lost 1
Martha Foss 1946 collision	Men lost 1
Mite 1954 weather	Men lost 2
Neptune 1949 tow - ship	Men lost 1
Nor'west 1951 fire	
Petrel 1952 weather - condition	Whole crew
Rivtow Rogue 1975 ?	Men lost 7
Ruby VIII 1949 ?	Men lost 2
Scotch Fir 1963 ?	Men lost 2
St . Clair 1949 weather	Men lost 3
Standard 1894 weather	Men lost 3?
Teeshoe 1954 ship weather	Men lost 4
Tornado 1965 tow	Men lost 1
Velos 1895 weather - tow	Men lost 4-5
W.H. McFadden 1947 weather	Men lost 8

The Sovereign, owned by Fremont Tugboat Co. Pusher-type tug. Lake Washington ship canal.

Seaspan Protector, twin screw, 1,400 hp. Used for general towing.
The high bows on these vessels were designed so the crew's quarters would be above the water line.

Haida Chieftain, European style of ocean-going tug though built in U.S. At this time she was owned by Shields Towing. The raised fore deck reduces the amount of solid water coming over the bow. Can make it safer to work on deck.

The Island Commander. She arrived on the coast as a steam trawler. She was later converted to a tug as many of these vessels were. Later she became a diesel. She had a long history on the coast working for several owners.

Ocean Master, Rivtow Straits. A large tug built for towing log barges. She towed large barges with supplies to northern British Columbia ports.

Gillnetters! I didn't see any. Has fishing season opened up yet?

Seaspan King. Built in 1968 for log barge work. Reg. length 122 ft. (37 m.) 3,225 hp.

The Seaspan Monarch docking a ship at Roberts Bank, reg. length 136 ft. (41 m.) 3,500 hp. Built in 1966.
She was originally the Harold A. Jones, Vancouver Tug. She towed salt barges from California as well as rock south.

The Seaspan Navigator.

Seaspan Warrior. The hull was built in the east coast and
then towed around to the west. Later an engine and
housework was added. Used a lot for towing on the west
coast of Vancouver Island.

A Kort Nozzle. This vessel has two non-steering nozzles
with large rudders behind them. Other vessels have nozzles that turn and steer the boat. You must have them
aiming the right direction when you go astern or you have
a bad landing.

The Seaspan Commodore a 157 ft. (48 m.) tug built for towing log barges but has the capability of towing world wide. She has 5,750 hp. so she can handle very large barges.

The Neva Straits. 86 ft. (26 m.) 1,320 hp.

The Commodore's towing winch. She has a double drum winch. Note the heavy chain that she can pull up on the winch. This chain is used for off-shore towing to add weight to gear. The size of the towline on vessels of this size can be seen on the starboard drum. When towing with a full line out she will have to stay outside the 35 fathom line or the towline could touch bottom.

The Sea Commander heading down river with an empty barge. The 150 ft.(46 m.) 3,060 hp. ex-U.S. Army tug is owned by Sea-Link Marine Services Ltd. These vessels had a high bow without the raised deck.

The after deck of the wooden, Island Monarch. The strong backs often called "Dutch Bars" are used on most traditional deep-sea tugs with a long after deck. They keep the towline off the deck. Capstans and wire lines are used to pull the heavy towline around. The rest of the towing gear is handled the same way.

The bows of tractor tugs usually have a different shaped bow than a conventional tug.

Modern Cates tug of the Z-peller type. A form of tractor tug. Note, Washington Marine Group logo that is replacing the older ones on a lot of B.C. tugs.

The Garth Foss, 8,000 hp. used for escorting tankers down Juan de Fuca Strait. She is a tractor tug designed to escort 125,000 dwt. tankers.

The Garth Foss towing winch. Note the synthetic line. Tugs such as these can tow off the bow as well as the stern which makes them efficient for ship work. They can not get into a girding position.

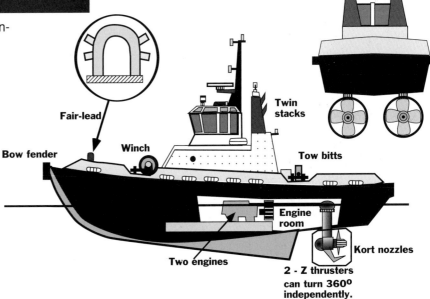

Diagram of a reverse-tractor tug. If the propulsion units are forward it is a tractor tug; if they are aft, it is a reverse-tractor tug. If used for ship work only, they will have a towing winch on the fore deck. If used for general towing, they may have a winch aft as well as a winch forward.

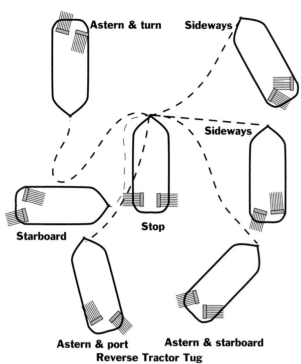

Astern & turn   Sideways

Sideways

Starboard   Stop

Astern & port   Astern & starboard
Reverse Tractor Tug

Small tug at Chemainus.

The concept of tug handling with a tractor tug is entirely different than that of a conventional vessel.

Westminster river boats used for ship docking and general river work.

The Seaspan Venture is a 1,440 hp. tug that can tow two chippers from the North Arm of Vancouver to Howe Sound ports in a single shift.

The Seaspan Rival is a single screw harbour tug. She has a steering nozzle.

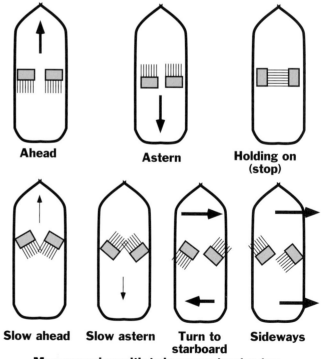

Ahead   Astern   Holding on (stop)

Slow ahead   Slow astern   Turn to starboard   Sideways
Manoeuvering with twin screw tractor tug

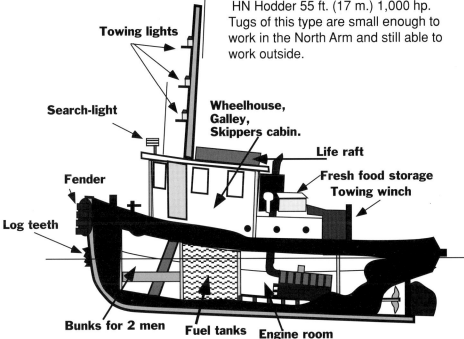

HN Hodder 55 ft. (17 m.) 1,000 hp. Tugs of this type are small enough to work in the North Arm and still able to work outside.

Towing lights

Search-light

Wheelhouse, Galley, Skippers cabin.

Life raft

Fender

Fresh food storage

Towing winch

Log teeth

Bunks for 2 men   **Fuel tanks**   **Engine room**

Harbour and river boats are designed to work in tight spaces and operate with a small crew. The power and size varies. The vessels designed for ship work usually have the most power. The American harbour boats are often bigger than the Canadian boats.

Left: Older type river boat used in the North Arm and Howe Sound. Boats of this type can be found in most coastal ports.

STEAM ENGINES

A tug is, in some respects, a floating power plant and fuel container. Today, we are familiar with 1,800 to 3,000 hp. tugs with some vessels having 7,000 hp. but at first, the boats were very low powered. It is hard to equate a steam engine turning a big, slow-turning wheel rated in nominal horsepower with a modern diesel-powered vessel, but some of the early propeller tugs probably had less than 100 horsepower. For years, no one expected tugs could move their tows very fast. This has certainly changed with modern tug and tow operations.

One of the early applications of the marine steam engine on the coast was in tugs. The first tugs were paddle-wheelers. The tugs started using screw propulsion as soon as reliable engines were available. Some of the problems associated with using a screw on large, wooden passenger and freight vessels did not affect the smaller tugs. Because of their manoeuvrability, tugs in Europe used paddlewheels

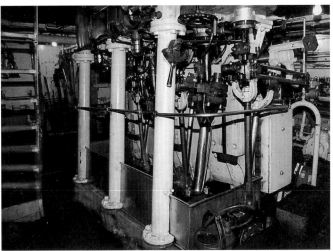

The Master's engine room. This is the type of engine room found on most steam tugs of this size. The boiler was fired from the forward end of the engine room.

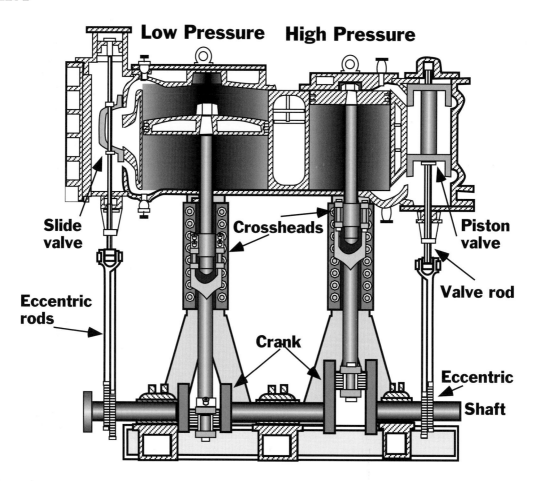

Low Pressure   High Pressure

Slide valve

Crossheads

Piston valve

Valve rod

Eccentric rods

Crank

Eccentric

Shaft

Compound steam engine. The steam is introduced to the high pressure piston valve. This valve lets steam into the high pressure cylinder on one side of the piston while exhausting steam from the other side. The exhausted steam goes to the slide valve on the other end of the engine. The steam then enters the low pressure cylinder. After it has done its work there, it is exhausted to the condenser. The steam is condensed back to water and the air is pumped out. The water is put back in the boiler after some of the impurities have been removed. The valves are controlled by the eccentrics on the main shaft. More cylinders can be added but the same principles apply.

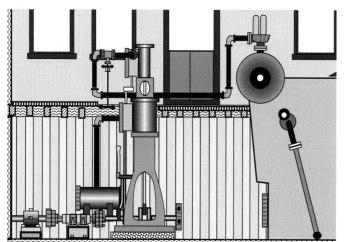

On small tugs that did not have room for the normal compound engine, a steeple compound was often used. With these engines the HP cylinder was placed over the LP cylinder. Having only one crank it had to be counter balanced. These engines were famous for getting stuck on top center. The engineer would have to shift the engine by hand with a bar on the flywheel.

in harbours for many years after they had disappeared on the west coast. They did not have to contend with dead-heads and driftwood.

It is hard to trace all the types of engines used in early tugs. The paddlewheel engines were sidelever, grasshopper, steeple and probably some vertical high-pressure engines. The vertical direct-acting engine was one of the first used in screw-type boats. As boiler pressure increased, compound and triple expansion engines were used. These engines and their boilers took up a lot of space so steeple compound and, at times, a quadruple expansion with only two cranks, were used.

Boilers varied but the most common was the scotch marine. Some boats had one of the many types of water-tube boilers. A small boat could be fitted with a vertical boiler. The water-tube boiler, while quicker to get steam up, needed careful firing and could not always supply enough steam for an extra load.

The inverted vertical direct-acting engine was so named because up to its introduction, most engines had the cylinder below or level with the shaft and a lot of them used levers or gears to get the power to the crank. On larger vessels more than one of these engines could be used on the same shaft. They originally operated on around 30 psi after surface condensers became practical. These engines were found on small tugs long after the bigger compound and triple expansion engines were the norm. As with all single-crank engines, they were easy to get stuck on top center; that is, the crank and the connecting rod are aligned when the engine is stopped. The engine can not go ahead or astern until the shaft is manually moved with a bar. If there is a bit of pressure in the cylinder, it can cause the bar to go flying when the engineer moves the shaft.

As steam pressures increased, the compound engine became practical. The steam is partly expanded in the high pressure cylinder before going to the low pressure cylinder where it is exhausted to the condenser. A vacuum is maintained in the condenser by an air pump. By the 1880s the boiler pressures had increased enough to make the triple expansion engine viable.

The problem with these large steam engines and boilers was they used a lot of fuel for the amount of horsepower produced and were also labour intensive.

At first they burnt wood which, while being readily available, was not an efficient fuel. When coal mines were established most started burning coal. There were still coal-burning tugs working in the early 1950s. Most switched to oil when it became available.

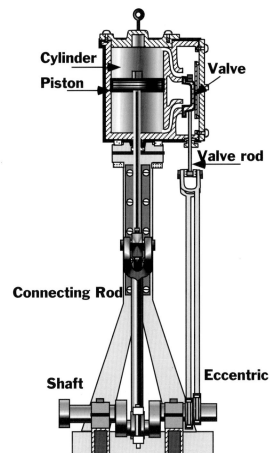

The vertical direct-acting steam engine. One of the earlier types of engines used on screw driven boats. They were used before compound engines were available on small tugs. They could use more than one of these engines on the same shaft. The Shamrock, 1887 had one of these engines before being repowered with a steeple.

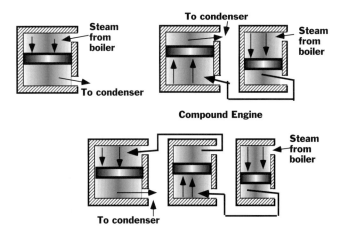

Above: Diagram showing how the steam was expanded on some types of engines.

Left: A small engine that was supposed to be out of a tug. To make the engine smaller, they used a quadruple expansion engine with the cylinders on top of each other. One crank for two cylinders. One valve shaft operated two valves. This type of engine was more common on larger ships.

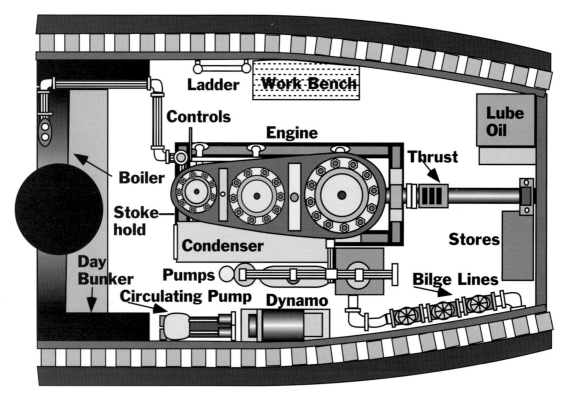

The engine room on a typical steam tug. Each tug was different as were their engines and other equipment. This engine room was a coal burner. The coal was trimmed aft to day bunkers on each side of the boiler. The bunkers would last a six hour watch. If it did not, the deck hand or fireman that did not manage to quite fill it, got up off watch and completed the job. There was no overtime paid in those days.

DIESEL ENGINES

The diesel engine eventually replaced the steam engine entirely on tugs and other coastal vessels. This happened in the United States sooner than Canada due to crewing regulations. In the United States, an engineer was often not required for a diesel where one would be required for the same sized engine in Canada. Over the years regulations have been constantly changing in both countries as to crew requirements. The companies that did not modernize and repower their tugs with diesel engines could not compete and disappeared.

The diesel is a type of internal combustion engine. The first successful engine of this kind was built by Dr. Rudolf Diesel in 1895. The diesel was used at first on smaller vessels, but in 1910 the first ocean-going tanker was fitted with a diesel. By the 1930s around 70 per cent of ships were diesel. Despite this, there were still steam tugs operating in the fifties.

The first marine diesels were not small engines for their horsepower. They took up a lot less space than a boiler and steam engine. Most of the earlier engines in tugs were semi-diesels.

The advantage of reduced crew requirements and increased horsepower made even the earliest diesels practical on some tugs. More electrical equipment was installed so batteries and auxiliary diesel engines became part of the engine room. Not all engineers were crazy about this fancy electrical stuff. The engine rooms also became a lot noisier.

As most of us deck department guys are not supposed to know one end of a wrench from the other (thank

The engine room on the Sirmack. The vessel had a large slow speed direct-reversible Fairbanks Morse engine. To go astern, the engineer stopped the engine and started it again in the astern position.

The engine room of the Island Mariner before she was repowered. She is a twin screw tug with each engine connected to a shaft through a reduction gear. The reduction gear reduces the RPM of the high speed diesels down to a much slower shaft speed. The engines operate in one direction as the engines use clutches for ahead and astern movements.

heaven), a small discussion of what a diesel is might be in order. In a diesel engine, air is compressed to a high temperature by a piston. Fuel is injected and ignited by the high temperature of the air. The expanding gases force the piston down. Diesels are either two-cycle or four-cycle engines. They can be double-acting or single-acting engines.

In the four-cycle engine, four strokes are required to draw in a change of air, compress it to a high pressure and temperature, inject and burn fuel, allow the gases to expand and deliver the power to the crankshaft. In a multi-cylinder-four-cycle engine all cylinders complete their cycle in two revolutions of the crankshaft.

The piston moves down from the top of the cylinder to the bottom during the intake stroke with the intake valve open to let in air. After the intake valve is closed, the piston moves upward on the compression stroke, compressing the air. Near the end of the compression stroke, fuel is injected into the hot air, vapourized and burned. The expanding high pressure gases force the piston down on the power stroke. Near the bottom, dead center, the exhaust valve is opened and the piston moves up on the exhaust stroke forcing the exhaust gases out.

I see the chief just learned that you do not connect batteries of opposite polarity.

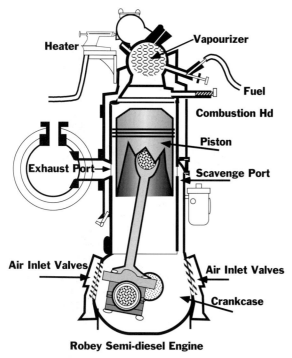

Robey Semi-diesel Engine

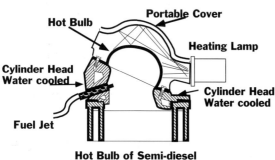

Hot Bulb of Semi-diesel

Some of the first diesel engines used were semi-diesels. They obtained ignition by using low compression and a hot cylinder head (hot bulb). The fuel is pumped against the hot cylinder cover to ignite it on compression. The compression on these engines is around 200 psi. A standard diesel engine uses a much higher pressure eliminating the need for a hot bulb.

Chief! the skipper wants to know if you are going to fix the engine in time for the next tide?

Two-stroke engines make use of exhaust and transfer (air) ports, rather than valves as on the four-cycle engines. On a two-stroke engine, air must be supplied under pressure by some other means, as each upward stroke of the engine is the compression stroke and each downward stroke is the power stroke. Intake and exhaust functions must take place while the piston is near the bottom of the cylinder. This can be done by a number of methods including a crankcase-scavenging method or a Uniflow (blower) method.

Theoretically, a two-cycle engine produces twice the horsepower of a four-cycle engine. It does not. It produces more horsepower for the same weight and bulk than the unsupercharged four-cycle engine.

Most two-cycle and four-cycle engines operate the cylinder air charge at the start of the compression stroke near atmospheric pressure. These are called atmospheric or normally-aspirated engines. On a two-cycle engine, if a blower is used to increase the air pressure at the start of compression, it is a supercharged engine. If, on an engine the blower is powered by the exhaust gases, it is turbocharged. Turbocharging can increase the power from 50 to over a 100 per cent on engines designed for this.

The semi-diesel engine was used in many tugs before it was replaced by the higher pressure pure diesel engine. These were not easy engines to operate but they made it possible to put more power in a tug in far less space.

The semi-diesel is a low pressure diesel that needs heating of a hot bulb for starting. After the engine is running, the heat of the gases will keep it operating without external heating. The fuel is injected under pressure to the top of the cylinder head. The heater vapourizes the fuel and the cylinder compresses the mixture of fuel and air till it ignites. The heater is turned off automatically on some engines and manually on others. The engineer must make sure the cylinder head does not get too hot or too cold.

The heavy duty, slow and medium speed engines eventually replaced these engines entirely. They were the direct-reversible type. That is, to go from ahead to astern the engine had to be stopped and the calms changed. The engine then had to be restarted. As air was used to restart the engine, the captain had to be careful not to run out of air.

On one 75 ft. fish packer equipped with a direct-reversible engine, the chief and the skipper had an argument at the ice plant. After telling the skipper he could run the engine by himself, the chief jumped off the boat and walked up the dock. As the skipper could start the engine from the wheelhouse (wheelhouse control) he departed for the company dock without "that damn engineer." He attempted his usual highball landing at the dock, but when he tried to put the engine astern he found he was out of air. Fortunately, the boat hit a solid bunch of pilings or it would have gone under the dock and removed its housework. The blow was hard enough to shake the two buildings on the wharf. Office workers started to evacuate in great haste thinking the old buildings were collapsing. The manager ran down to the dock to survey the damage and have a chat with the skipper. While this was going on the engineer arrived by taxi. After boarding the boat he started the engine without checking to see if the clutch was engaged. It was. The boat lunged forward breaking her lines. As the rest of the crew was on the dock, the mate and deck hand had to make a jump for the rigging to get on board. The mate got the boat under control before it hit a nearby bridge. The manager and the skipper renewed their earnest discussion.

There were many makes of these engines installed in tugs. Some replaced steam engines and others were put into new hulls. During the depression, there was not an awful lot of new construction going on. One make of engine that was successfully used was the "Enterprise" an inline four cycle, slow speed engine. A lot of tugs built for the U.S. service during the war and used by towboat companies on both sides of the border, were equipped with Fairbanks Morse engines. Washington engines were used in some tugs as were Cooper-Bessemers, Union and Atlas Imperial. Early models of the Caterpillar were used on smaller tugs.

In the 1960s high speed turbocharged engines came into general use. This changed the entire towboat industry. A far greater amount of power could be put into a smaller hull with a smaller crew. At first, these engines were put in existing (often wooden) hulls, but new designs of tugs were launched to take advantage of these engines. The need for electricity increased, batteries became redundant and auxiliaries were installed to run 24 hours a day. With the use of all this turbocharged power, the noise on board increased dramatically. This was not just a problem in the engine room. Skippers found that crews could not hear orders twenty feet away no matter how hard they shouted. This became a bad safety hazard. Crews were starting to have hearing problems. To overcome this, newer boats were built with reduced sound levels. Some of the older boats had sound reduction systems installed.

The noise is dispersed throughout the boat from the engine beds to the rest of the vessel. Engines were mounted on newer-type engine mounts to reduce this problem. The noise problem has been reduced dramatically today.

These faster-turning engines had to have reduction gears fitted between the engine and the propeller shaft. For maximum efficiency when pulling, the propeller must be large and relatively slow turning. If a small, fast turning propeller was used, the propeller would cavitate rendering it almost useless. Hydraulically activated clutches were installed that decreased the time in going from ahead to astern. The controls from steering station to clutch were improved. Some of these were operated by air. This, along with power steering, meant that it was relatively easy to have several stations from where the vessel could be handled.

All this modern equipment did not alleviate all problems. A tug going into a pulp mill in Howe Sound with a car barge loaded with chemicals picked up her barge alongside. She started her approach to the rail slip at half speed. Suddenly, the helm indicator stopped working. The steering had gone. The skipper went astern. Nothing happened. The variable-pitch propeller had packed it in. The engineer came up and said the steering motor and the propeller were out and the skipper had better do something. Without steering or power there was not much that could be done. The skipper radioed a small tug for immediate assistance. The rail slip was getting closer all the time. If the barge hit it at speed, the rail cars of chemicals could rup-

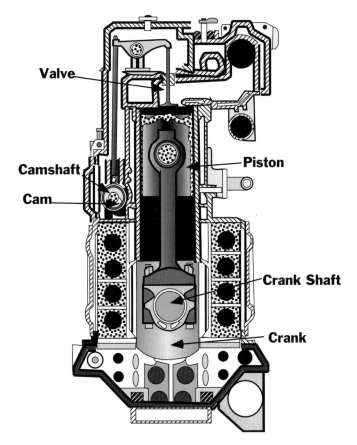

Cross section of a slow speed direct-reversible engine. This type of engine was used in tugs for years. Below: Electrical panel, Island Mariner.

An Enterprise Diesel manufactured by the Enterprise Engine and Machinery Co. This make of slow speed engine was used in many tugs.
Oregon Maritime Center and Museum, Portland.

Engine, Seaspan Valiant. This 850 hp. engine is far smaller than the 400 hp. engine in the Sirmac. She has a variable pitch propeller and a Kort nozzle.

ture. Just as things were getting to the panicky state, the barge turned about a hundred degrees on its own. The barge and boat drifted down the bay till the small boat could get to them.

Some tugs do not have engineers. The requirement for having licensed or certified engineers on tugs is quite different in the U.S. and Canada. Union agreements can also have a bearing on engine room manning. On many American boats a seaman that has passed the Coast Guard qualifications will look after the machinery.

On Canadian boats it is usually the skipper or the mate that takes over the engineering duties. On a small log-tower running light, working north of Prince Rupert, the engine quit. The mate was called to fix it. The skipper informed the sleepy-eyed mate that they were close to shore and there was a big swell running. It was further

pointed out that if the tug drifted on to shore the old bucket would quickly break up in the breakers. The mate found that the fuel filters had plugged. He changed filters in record time as the boat rolled around. After pumping fuel through the system to avoid an air lock, he hit the start button on each engine. They both started. By the time he got on deck they were pulling off the beach which, by this time, was a bit close.

On these vessels other machinery such as towing winches can be operated from the after station. Hydraulically operated towing pins and, on some vessels the tie-down gear, can be operated from the same location. On some harbour tugs winches for the deck lines can be operated from the wheelhouse. This enables the skipper to position his tug where he wants it when he is made up to a barge or ship. All these improvements meant that a tug could handle increasingly bigger tows.

When fuel became very expensive some of the boats had their speeds reduced. Computers were installed on some vessels to monitor the fuel consumption and adjust speed accordingly. The problem with reducing speed meant it was easy to get the engine on a "critical." A critical speed is when the engine speed causes an abnormal vibration which can damage the engine. The engine makers started to design engines with greater fuel efficiency. Older engines were often replaced with these fuel efficient engines.

When new tugs are built, higher horsepower engines are usually installed. As the demands on the tug increase, this trend will probably continue.

The skipper was wondering if you noticed that he forgot and went full ahead while you were working on the engine.

2
THE TOWBOAT MEN

Captain Micky Dickson at the after controls of the Island Mariner. The engine controls are by his right hand. At the time this photograph was taken most of the towing winch controls were on deck.

THE CREWS

Towboat crews anywhere in the world are a specialized type of seamen. When sailing vessels were still around, they were often known as steamboat men. They require all the skills of any seaman plus the ability to work with tows much larger than their own vessel. The crew on a tug boat is small and versatile. The deck crew must be very agile in order to move around their tows in less than appealing conditions.

As with any trade, the industry has its own jargon. Some of the terms are unique to the industry such as "picking up a barge" or "making up to a barge." A lot of the terms have come down through the ages. You may hear someone say the tug is "backing and filling" when the boat is going ahead and astern in order to turn the boat in a short distance. This, of course, is a term left over from the days of sail. Today, you are not supposed to say starboard or port when giving helm orders. To be politically correct you do not call a ship a she. Unfortunately, in time, all the seagoing terms will be gone.

Navigating a tug and tow around the coast was not easy. When the first tugs started working the west coast of North America, there were none of the aids to navigation or electronics that everyone depends on today. It is hard to imagine what it must have been like to tow a slow moving log boom when you did not know how the tides were going to affect you or even where all the rocks were. The towboat skippers and mates soon developed local knowledge and a unique ability to navigate their heavy tows around the coast.

The skipper or mate needed to be able to pick out the faint loom of land and any sounds coming out of the night. In the dark you would "lose your eyes," night vision, if you turned on a light to look at the chart. Charts were often not kept in the very small wheelhouses for this reason. A dim, red light will not affect night vision as much as a white light so, in later years, a small, red light or a flashlight with a red covering over the lens was used for chart work.

The wheelhouse windows were raised or lowered with a leather strap attached to the bottom of the window.

Deck hand splicing deck line. Most of the gear is made up ashore now. On the steam tugs most of the rigging work was done aboard.

Rope fenders were made from old rope. The worn out manila couplers made good fenders.

Windows in the up position were jammed with wooden wedges so they would not rattle. In poor visibility they tried not to "look through glass" so one window was usually down or partly down at all times. In narrow passes, the windows were hauled up and down on opposite sides of the wheelhouse as the skipper or mate tried to pick out some sight of land.

In good weather or bad, courses were steered with as much accuracy as possible. New seamen were taught by the mate to "box the compass" and steer as soon as they came aboard. If a new hand did not pick this up very quickly, it was often more than the compass that was "boxed." The skipper or mate periodically checked the compass to make sure the seaman was on course at all times. If the seaman was out of the wheelhouse, the skipper or mate could keep an accurate course while looking out the open window by viewing the compass from the side. At night, the compass binnacle light was kept very dim and often red in colour in order not to reflect too much light around the wheelhouse.

It is not just the skippers and mates that need towboat experience. A deck hand must be able to tie up barges, get the gear ready for any job and handle boom chains often without supervision. Under the mate's supervision, he must know how to maintain a lot of equipment, steer and keep a lookout. The engineers and cooks had an equally important part of keeping the vessel operating smoothly. The industry eventually expanded into specialized areas, such as harbours, rivers, coastal and offshore. Each part of the industry developed people with skills in that particular endeavour. The crews that work the small river boats must have a lot of local knowledge along with the ability to handle the tows in the strong river currents. The logtowers learn the regions they normally work in and ask questions if they get a tow from a strange area. The crews on the tugs that specialize in barge towing develop an ability to handle large barges in a variety of conditions as well as tow them in heavy weather. Some crews work on the ocean-going tugs that tow large barges or ships to many places in the world. These are not usually coastal seamen. Until recent times a lot of men would work for a variety of companies in order to increase experience. Regardless of the type of work the tug is doing, the skipper's ability to manoeuvre the tug is extremely important. Steam tugs were not as easy to handle as the modern tug with all the nice little levers for steering. The big wheel had to be turned by hand to get a big rudder from hard over one way to hard over the other. As with all endeavours, some men are naturally better at handling a boat than others. There are not very many towboat skippers that can not handle a boat well. There are, however, a number of ex-skippers that can not handle a boat. The number of ships' pilots that come from the towboat industry attest to the vast shipping and coastal knowledge that the tug boat skippers and mates have.

As on any work vessel, there is a definite order of command and responsibility on a tug. The captain is responsible for the tug, the crew and the tow. At one time, he could hire and fire without much argument from anyone. Many a deck hand that had to find his own way home from some out of the way place can attest to that.

The mate is the next man down in the deck department. At one time, a lot of the mates were uncertified. The mate was picked by the master for his ability and willingness to work. The mate, in addition to navigational duties, is responsible for the upkeep of the towing gear and the tug. When crews were larger, there was an awful lot of scraping and painting to be done. It was the mate's job to organize the work for the seamen. If the tug was tied up waiting weather, he would also be out with scraper and brush. As mates were assigned to a boat for a long time, there was a lot of rivalry between them as to which boat looked the best.

Now most mates are certified and learn their navigation in school. They often have a higher academic standard than in earlier times.

A good seaman is experienced, knowledgeable, hard working and worth his weight in gold. Usually a deck hand started out on the mate's watch to learn the basics from the mate. He learned to steer, handle lines and chains. As time went on, he learned how to splice and make rope fenders. He soon became acquainted with painting and scraping. In a short time, he could work out on the scows or the booms without supervision. When he had mastered these tasks, he would be put on the skipper's watch to start learning his way around the coast. He was in training for a mate's job. He increasingly learned about other necessary skills required and was taught to be self-reliant and given the opportunity to make some decisions but always under the skipper's or mate's watchful eye. As wages improved and opportunities decreased, a lot of men made a career of being seamen on larger ships. With smaller crews today, the seaman may learn more about cooking than navigation.

The engineers are a very necessary part of the crew. In the steamboat era, there were at least two engineers and a fireman. Larger tugs had additional firemen as well as coal passers. The chief is the officer in charge. Under him there is a second, and in some cases, a third engineer. The firemen and oilers work under their direction. In addition to sea time, it takes a lot of study and hard work to qualify for the various engineers' certificates.

When oil was introduced, the firemen disappeared except on the very large tugs. The engineers on steamboats were always busy. In addition to handling the engine when manoeuvring, they were constantly adjusting and repairing equipment. When the annual overhaul was taking place, they did most of the work with the aid of shorefitters. Without their constant attention the boats would not have gone very far.

The cook is the other member of the crew that can not be forgotten. A good cook can make a terrible trip bearable. A bad cook can reduce morale faster than any one man on the boat. It is not only his ability to cook but his attitude in the galley when the crew comes in wet and tired. On the old boats he seemed to always produce a good meal despite limited resources.

On a lot of the old boats, the cook called the daylight watches with a large bell. He would ring it with vigour in the fo'c'sel or wherever there was anyone sleeping. Some of these bells are now on the bottom of the ocean.

Towboats were, and still are, good feeders. The meals were better on tugs than a lot of coastal freighters. Most steamboats only had an icebox to store fresh meat. Vegetables were stored in lockers on the boat deck. As the boats were often out for long periods, keeping fresh food was a problem. On the logtowers, they used to hang the

The mate at the wheel.

The mate on the Seaspan Valiant. The wheelhouse on modern vessels is far easier to work in.

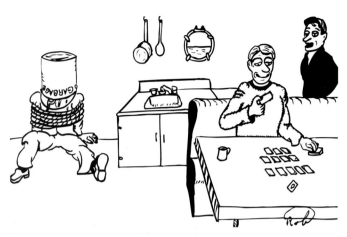

I see the cook has been telling you what moves you missed again chief.

Mate on the Seaspan Valiant handling the boat from the after controls. He could steer, control the engine, operate the towing winch and the pins from this location. The mate on these vessels used to stand watch by himself. He had to be able to take barges off other tugs as well as all the wheel duties such as navigation and keeping a lookout for traffic. The engineer had the same watch and could help a bit. Now, on this vessel, there is a deck hand on watch with the mate but there is no engineer on board.

Before the 1970s the mate on a one deck hand boat often was by himself for his six-hour watch. The engineer was on watch with the skipper.

On the bigger boats there were two deck hands so one of them stood the twelve-to-six watch with the mate.

meat up and cut a piece off when needed. Then, as now, it is always a challenge to get a good meal out when the boat is rolling and pitching. Today, in order to reduce costs and make the vessel more competitive, cook deck hands are replacing cooks.

While a lot of Canadian harbour boats work shifts of eight or twelve hours, the outside boats all stand watches so the boat can operate twenty-four hours a day. On Canadian boats the watches are six hours on and six hours off. The mate gets the twelve-to-six watch and the skipper the six-to-twelve watch. If there are two engineers, the chief stands the same watch as the master. On large tugs with a second mate, the master does not have a watch. The first mate still stands the twelve-to-six and the second mate has the six-to-twelve watch. The engineers work the same way if there is a large crew.

On American boats they have the same system in Puget Sound and local waters but for the longer runs, the Coast Guard requires they work four hours on and eight hours off. On a number of harbour boats, the crew stays on the boat for days. They stand watches the same way the outside boats do.

The Fraser River logboats work the tides. Tows go up river on the flood and down river on the ebb. The tows have to be yarded before slack water. At one time, this usually meant the crews did not get too much sleep. Regardless of the type of tug, the crews on the older tugs would work off watch whenever needed. For years there was no overtime pay so calling out the off-watch crowd was no big deal. On Canadian vessels there are now limits to the number of hours a man can work.

Time off the tug was hard to get in the thirties. The only way a crew member got time off was to find someone to replace him and then try and talk him into getting off when the crew member came back. There was no pay while you were off. A three month trip was common. The crew took every opportunity to get ashore when the tug got into a port. The companies tried to keep the men from getting home when they got into port unless the tug was not needed.

The U.S. boats in the Sound got day-for-day long before the Canadian tugs but eventually everyone got time off. In order to make up for the standard twelve hour day, Canadian crews get 1.4 days off for every day worked. The length of time on the tug varies with the company and where it is working. A lot of crews working on short coastal runs will get off every two weeks. American vessels on long runs will have three month or longer trips and, as they stand four and eight watches, do not get day-for-day.

Ultimately, overtime was paid for working over the twelve hours. This was unheard of in most companies until the fifties. When the boats became more powerful and communications improved, the crews were often worked till they dropped especially on the smaller boats. Before the hours of work legislation, fatigue created a lot of accidents.

The living conditions on tugs over the years have ranged from terrible to excellent. Until WWII, crews packed their own bedding on many boats.

On a large modern tug, the crew will have pleasant rooms, big mess room/galley, showers, washing machines and room to stow personal gear. On some of the smaller boats, especially those operating in the sixties, the conditions were poor. The skipper often slept in the wheelhouse/galley while the rest of the crew slept in an unheated, damp fo'c'sel. It was hard to dry clothes and the bedding was constantly damp or wet. There was very little chance of getting out alive if the boat started to sink. A number of men went down on these boats until government and union regulations changed the way these vessels could operate.

While the earlier towboat men did not get much time off, the lack of modern radio communication and the fact that a lot of the tows would not take much weather, meant that things went at a considerably slower pace than they do today. If the boat got into a port, the crew would try to get ashore for a few hours. The men worked together for long periods and built up a comradeship and long-lasting friendships.

Before much time off was available, the crews would often take the opportunity to have a glass if they got a few hours ashore. There is a story that we can not verify about a tug backing out from the dock in Vancouver after the crew had been ashore. The skipper was balanced with one foot in the wheelhouse and the other on the rail so he could see astern. He fell over the side and the boat backed out without him. The crew had to bring the tug back to pick him up. Now all liquor is strictly forbidden. Anyone coming aboard drunk is likely to have his employment terminated.

Since radios came in, a tug might not even complete a voyage before orders are changed. If the weather is not good enough to tow logs, the boat can be off towing scows.

On the wooden boats the decks were often hard to keep watertight so the fo'c'sel could get damp. On the wooden steamboats there was lots of heat to eventually dry things out and the deck-heads did not sweat like the steel hulls. If you had a cabin on deck, you could stay warm and dry. As the housework was usually made of tongue and grove planks, water could squirt between the cracks in heavy weather. The galleys were small and had minimal equipment.

On the older wooden tugs there were often no inside passages. This meant you would likely get wet if you went from place to place in bad weather. As the ladder to the top deck and the wheelhouse was usually located forward, you had to move fast if you wanted to get to the wheelhouse dry. It paid to stick your head out the galley door till it looked like there was a small sea coming, then run for it. This strategy was not guaranteed to work. On the larger ocean-going tugs, there were some inside passages. When the larger steel boats came along, they were usually designed with inside passages.

When the crew was off watch, cards were often played. If a logboat was tied up waiting weather, the crew would often wander out on the boom or go ashore. At times they would find oysters. Fishing was often successful on the longer tows. Most boats had long poles they could put out to keep the lines away from the wheel wash.

The crews did most of the vessels' maintenance. Brass was kept polished and paint and decks were washed. In summer the whole tug would be scraped and painted. At one time, most of the gear was spliced on board. Big rope fenders were made from old manila (rope) couplers.

As the size of the crews has decreased while the size of the tows has increased, the crews do not have time

Captain Jim Dean on the Island Trooper. He later went into the office and eventually ran Seaspan's Victoria office.

The mate and the deck hand have to pull the heavy log gear aboard at the end of a tow. They have to place all the gear on the boom before departing with the tow and may have to go out on the booms to make repairs at any time of the day or night, whether on watch or off.

Deck hand washing the paintwork. The crew keeps the boat clean. At times the outside may not look as well as one would like but the crew's quarters are kept spotless.

to do as much maintenance as in earlier times. Most of the work is done by shore crews when the vessel is in port.

While there are some women on the boats, it is still very much a male-dominated job. Most women seem to find the heavy gear and working conditions not too enjoyable on a long-term basis. However, there have been several female skippers over the years. As time goes on, there may be more opportunities in the future.

If the forest industry keeps declining on the coast, employment on the tugs will probably decline. It takes much longer today to get a promotion regardless of qualifications.

As a new mate the first thing to learn is that if I put the boat aground it is due to extenuating circumstances. If you put it aground it's due to plain stupidity.

The deck hands and mates must be very good at handling lines and wire bridles. Barges and boats do not stay still too long so the crew has to be quick. A lot of the gear is heavier than this.
Left: Getting the bridles on the scow. The boat backs up to the scow and the crewman must get the bridles on quickly.

THE NAVIGATORS

Navigating the inside passage anywhere between Puget Sound and southeastern Alaska requires special skills. The tidal currents and winds are often strong and changeable. There are many deep inlets where soundings are not practical and there may be deep water next to a rock bluff or reef. Visibility can be poor due to heavy rain or fog.

The conditions on the coast produced a specialized type of seaman. The ships' deck officers came from different backgrounds. The main categories were deep water, coastal passenger/freight, tug boat and fishing navigators.

The deep-water navigator was very good at mathematics and had the ability to find his way round the world by observing the sun and stars. He was usually not happy working close to shore

In the winter time on the coast, snow and gale force winds can be a problem especially farther north. An old steam tug headed to Union Bay with two empty coal scows and ran into a snow storm and S.E. gale. The skipper could not find Chrome Island, usually called "yellow rock," at the entrance to Baynes Sound. The snow had deadened the sound of the foghorn. She lay to all night in the gulf. The old type aerial blew off making the radio useless. Due to the heavy sea conditions, she had to have two men on the wheel to steer her. The skipper could only guess her position until he got a break in the weather some twelve hours later.

Disasters created when vessels hit a rock in poor visibility were numerous. In 1947, the passenger vessel, Gulf Stream, hit Dinner Rock with much loss of life. In 1953, the tug, C.P. York, hit Tattenham Reef in thick weather. The barge she was towing hit the stranded tug rolling it over and drowning seven of her crew.

Despite the fact that the Strait of Georgia is inside waters, many tugs and small passenger vessels were overwhelmed by the storms with the loss of many crews. Strong currents running against the waves create a very dangerous sea condition. Cape Mudge, at the north end of the Strait, is extremely dangerous in a flood tide and a S.E. gale. Several vessels have disappeared there. Queen Charlotte Sound, Hecate Strait and Dixon Entrance have open-ocean seas, strong currents and poor visibility. In addition, parts of these areas are shallow making a steep, dangerous sea.

When the navigator was in the passages and inlets of the area, local knowledge was even more important than on the outer coast. Most companies required their masters sail as mates in areas in which they were not familiar.

BEFORE ELECTRONICS

It is hard to imagine in this day of electronics how vessels navigated around the coast without them in the extremely competitive world of commercial transport. The time required to get from one port to another was, and still is today, one of the major concerns of vessel owners and masters. Passenger vessels and, to some extent, coastal freighters have a schedule to keep. For years the fastest ship got the business. Tugs, in most cases, do not have as firm an agenda. If the tug is on a car-barge or freight run, she has to try to arrive at her ports of call on time. There is still a lot of pressure on the company and the tug to deliver a

A deck hand getting ready to get up on an empty. When switching scows the seaman has to get up on the scows quickly. In bad weather and the middle of the night this is not easy.

On the older tugs the winch often did not have spooling gear. Spooling the towline was done with an iron bar.

Captain Adrian Bull at the after station of the Sudbury II. The master of an offshore tug must not only be a good ship handler, he must be able to take the tug and tow anywhere in the world. He must be able to get a line up on a ship at sea in a gale without damaging the tug or the ship.

The skippers in Vancouver Harbour often work with several boats at a time. The traffic is always busy.

tow as quickly as possible. Fish-packers must deliver their fish on time or lose valuable cargo. The navigator had to meet all these demands in addition to just getting his vessel from one port to another. Wind, sea conditions, current and visibility all have to be taken into account when making navigational decisions.

Regardless of the size of the vessel, wind and sea conditions affect speed. Smaller coastal vessels and tugs with tows may have to avoid heavy weather conditions entirely. The skipper may plan his trip to take advantage of protected waters or stay near inlets or islands where he can get out of the weather. The vessel's speed through the water, its draught and the difficulty of manoeuvring will make a difference as to where the vessel can go. Skippers with log tows have to constantly evaluate weather, current and available shelter.

Visibility is still a major factor in vessel operations. The rules of the road take this into account despite all the aids to navigation we have today. Before modern aids to navigation, black nights, rain, snow, mist and fog were major obstacles to a fast and safe voyage.

The other element that affects all coastal shipping is current. There are many narrows that a vessel can not proceed through against the current regardless of size or power. The speed of the trip will greatly depend on the master's ability to take advantage of fair tides and work the back eddies when bucking the tide. Current affects the ability of the vessel to stay on a given track over the bottom. The current running against the sea can produce dangerous sea conditions.

When working the coast, experience is the best tool in overcoming these difficulties. This means more than relying on a good memory though this certainly helps. Log books, sailing directories, tide books and the captain's black book are all used.

In order to understand earlier forms of coastal navigation, we must understand the equipment and conditions available to the masters and mates.

As you may have noticed from old photographs, the wheelhouses of the old ships of all sizes, including tugs, were very small. Often the wheel, binnacle, telegraph and a small shelf for the log book took up most of the space in the wheelhouse. The idea may have stemmed from the sailing ship personnel who considered wheelhouses were for sissies.

Until dynamos were installed in the late 19th century, there were no electric lights or searchlights. The first U.S. vessel to have electric lights was in 1879. While the odd ship may have had a carbon arc light, there were no searchlights as we know them for some years after that. The early dynamos were not noted for the amount of electricity they produced. If you kept the searchlight on too long, the engine room would start complaining. Until well into the 20th century most vessels did not have radios.

Of course magnetic compasses were the only ones used until gyro-compasses became available. Due to their size and power requirements, gyros were reserved for the larger vessels for many years. On tugs there would be a large compass in the wheelhouse. An additional compass, the standard compass, was located on the "monkey's island" (top of the wheelhouse) on coastal passenger and freight vessels.

Crew's quarters on the Nitinat Chief. The whole crew slept in the fo'c'sel. Boats of this size now would have separate rooms in most cases.

Gear is often stowed below. The crew have to bring it up on deck before the job starts and stow it again.

Office, this is Little Shove III. The cook is quitting. Would you send us a new cook and be sure and send the ten pounds of coffee this one forgot to order.

The cook is always busy. The crew depend on him to have a hot meal even if the boat has been rolling around in heavy sea.

Left: The skipper always has mounds of paperwork. Customs' papers, logs and reports have to be written, often off watch.

I think now would be a good time to hold a safety meeting.

Captain Jack Hamilton on the Nitinat Chief. Boats such as this with the direct-reversible engines were not as handy as the newer vessels.
Below: Capt. MacGillivary yarding logs.

Charts were expensive and not always reliable. While Captain Vancouver did a general survey of the west coast of North America in 1792, inshore charts were unreliable. The aids to navigation were scarce for years. Due to lack of room, many vessels did not have a chart table in the wheelhouse. The charts were often stowed in the captain's cabin or, on some larger ships, in a chart room just aft of the wheelhouse.

With the limitations on navigational equipment and aids to navigation, local knowledge was very important. The skipper or mate would take advantage of good weather to pick out "marks." These might consist of a mountain top that could be seen on a dark night, a lower mark that could be identified if cloud covered the hills, range marks or where you would be on a position line if you could see a rock or island "open up" past a headland. You would know that if your bearing on a mountain top was correct you would clear a rock or reef that could not be picked up in poor visibility. The importance of identifying the skyline of harbour entrances was so great, that drawings of the hills and mountains were often located on earlier Admiralty Charts and in sailing directories. The captains and mates kept notes of some of the more important ones in their "black books." While in port skippers and mates would often take soundings from a small boat.

The coastal ships depended on the consistent running of courses and times. In good weather the courses and distance-off points were kept in the pilot house log. The navigator knew how long it should take him to reach a point or island. In poor visibility, if you did not pick up the point when you expected, it was time to slow down and try and establish a position. One of the first things a young officer had to learn was to rely on his compass.

This was not the only thing the navigator relied on. The steamships were quiet so you could hear the echo of the whistle. The steep bluffs in the inlets echoed the sound very well while the sandy beaches did not. A log close at hand would often return an echo. The distance off could be judged by the time it took for the echo to return. The speed of sound depends on the temperature. At 55° F. sound travels 1,116 feet per second. There are 6,080 feet to the nautical mile so if the echo took 2.75 sec. to return, the object was about a quarter of a mile off. The skippers and mates became proficient at estimating distances off without any timing device.

If you were going down a part of the coast with distinct drop-offs, such as parts of Juan de Fuca Strait, you could follow a single depth such as a 10 fathom line. This, along with your estimated speed over the bottom, would give you a reasonable idea of where you were until you could pick up something such as a foghorn. If you were crossing the contours, you could compare your soundings with the chart. Again, you would use your estimated speed over the bottom.

The log could be used in open water to give you a speed through the water. You had to use your local knowledge to estimate, due to current, the set (distance off course due to wind and current).

There always could be surprises and the fog could play tricks on the navigator. A new mate on a tug was heading down the middle of Juan de Fuca Strait bound for Point Wilson when what appeared to be a lighthouse showed up in the fog. As there were not supposed to be any lighthouses for miles, a feeling of panic started to set in. It turned out to be an aircraft carrier with the hull still enveloped in fog.

The direction of sound from a ship's whistle could be unreliable. Sound in fog could be very misleading so it always paid to hear a fog signal several times before making a move.

The tug boat crews developed special skills. Each type of tow and each area created special problems. For this reason more than one method of navigation was used in a given set of circumstances.

BARGE TOWING

When towing barges and scows, a tug was navigated in a similar manner to a coastal freighter. However, the tug operated at a much slower speed than a freighter so the effect of set due to current was far greater. The tug could not stop if an unfamiliar piece of land showed up or the tow would hit or pass it. As tows often varied, it was hard to estimate the speed until the tug had the tow for some hours.

Courses and times were logged as carefully in good weather as in poor. The state of the tide and weather were also logged along with the information about the tow. Courses were usually set between points or lights that could be identified in reduced visibility or at night. By keeping the same course, in poor visibility you had a better chance of arriving at the next point at the right distance off. This worked better than just taking the course off the chart as it took into account the current sets. In poor visibility you would run your course and you should pick up (find) the next point near the expected time. If you did not, it was time to find out why, if practicable. If possible, you would not pass major points or lights without identifying them.

As an example of this type of navigation, the Spray was entering Victoria Harbour at night towing a scow-load of scrap paper when the fog suddenly rolled in. Lookouts were posted on the bow. She entered the harbour on a slow bell (slow speed) and set a course for the BK beacon, the first light inside the breakwater. She picked up the light and set a course for the inner harbour. The echoes from the steam whistle told the skipper she was staying in the center of the channel. She picked up the beacon and rounded it landing her tow at the old Sidney Roofing paper dock. After making the scow fast, she departed for the Blackball dock still in thick fog. They talked to someone who said he was on the fisheries dock which gave them a position. When approaching the CPR dock the watchman on one of the ships started to ring a gong. The watchman told the tug which end of the dock he was on. The crew had not seen a thing since leaving Sidney Roofing. The tug altered course while trying to get an echo off the Blackball dock. She carefully approached where the echo seemed to be the strongest and found the dock when it was about ten feet off. Of course, things did not work out this well all the time and quite a few boats went aground.

Captain Bruce McDonald at the controls of the Seaspan Rascal. Handling a tug requires a lot of skill. This is not something that can be picked up from a book. Each boat and each operation is different. Handling a harbour or river boat is not the same as a big or medium size boat.

Didn't wait for slack water in the narrows again Cap.

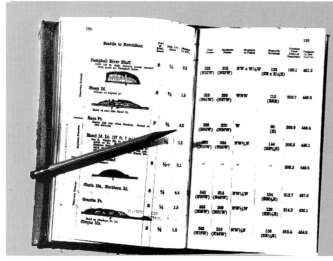

Captain Hansen's and Captain Lily's books had courses and distances worked out for the coastal navigator. These were not as useful to the coast hugging towboat navigators as they were to other vessels.

The chart, parallel rules, tide book and log book were the main navigation tools on tugs for years

Below: A good pair of binoculars and the lead line were also absolutely necessary. Right: A candle. The lighting often used along with whale oil before petroleum and electricity.

LOG TOWING

The logtower operated in a totally different environment. His tow was so heavy that courses and times were almost useless in poor visibility. He often had the advantage of being able to work very close to shore where he could pick up familiar parts of the beach. They were sometimes known as "kelp dodgers" because when the kelp showed up they pulled out into deeper water. Kelp is a seaweed that attaches itself to most rocks on the bottom. In more northerly waters it grows in 35 feet of water or less. Unfortunately, it breaks loose in the fall so is not there in the winter time.

If fog set in during a haul across the Strait of Georgia, you were working mainly by guess. When radio came in you often could get an approximate position from a passing vessel. On dark, rainy nights the skipper or mate would try to make his position from studying the skyline and picking up the beach on the searchlight.

The logtower always had to work with the currents. Slack water is slack water regardless of the visibility. If the tug and tow was not where it should be when the tide changed, it could be in serious trouble.

Even in good visibility the navigator had to work with the currents and the weather. If he was underway with a big, fair tide and the wind came up or the visibility disintegrated, he probably could not turn around and there may not be any safe harbours he could get into. These were some of the considerations that had to be taken into account before departing. Electronics improved the visibility factor, but the current and weather problem is still the same.

RIVER TOWING

Working in the river is a special type of work. The river is not a place to depend on courses and times. The old skipper had to know the area he was working in like the back of his hand. He had to know how river and tidal currents affected each bend and bar. Eventually the main channels were dredged and aids to navigation installed. Smaller channels and sloughs are often unmarked. The buoys can be out of place due to current or because other tows hung up on them. Traffic is often heavy so you must know how far you can go from the center of the channel. If the fog drifted in without warning, it could be quite entertaining.

ELECTRONIC NAVIGATION

When radar came in for the larger tugs, it started to change the industry. While large ships had radar earlier, most tugs did not start getting it until the fifties. The first radars were large boxes of tubes. They were all head-up types, that is, the vessel is in the center of the screen and the top is the direction she is heading. The screen was quite small and needed a magnifying glass to see the targets. The small logtowers and river boats did not have enough space or electrical power for these machines.

The crews were not too well trained on the new radar sets. At first, some of the skippers would not let the

A modern wheelhouse on a medium size tug.

mate operate them. Some were scared of them and others should have been. One skipper thought he could repair them as well as any technician until one dark night while adjusting the set with a brass-handled screwdriver, he hit the wrong part. There was a blinding flash, the skipper was flat on his back, a quarter of an inch of the screw driver was gone and several trays of tubes were toast.

As the radar sets became more compact nearly every boat had one. Now most tugs have two in case one fails.

The use of radar made the tugs far more productive. You could keep going regardless of visability. While local knowledge is still important, you need less of it in a lot of areas. Dark nights in the inlets are far easier to navigate. Collision avoidance systems have also been improved.

The radios in the wheelhouse have also improved navigation. The officer on watch can communicate with other vessels in the area about unexpected hazards.

The traffic control systems are a great aid to navigation. Not only do they prevent collisions, they can often warn the ship if it is heading into danger. However, the master should not depend too much on traffic control to keep him out of trouble. Some contend that traffic should have warned the Exxon Valdez before she went aground.

The tug or ship has to report to traffic before departing port, before entering a controlled zone from sea and at various reporting points along the route. The vessel is under radar surveillance in a lot of areas.

Most tugs today have radar and other electronic aids to navigation. They have increased the navigator's ability to estimate his position at all times. However, they are just aids to navigation and have their own errors. Even the GPS navigation systems have their errors.

Hey skipper! It's 03:00. The mate says you may want to get up as we are a bit handy to some lighthouse. The lighthouse keeper would like a word with you about damage to his paint.

The skipper and deck hand. Before auto pilots the seaman steered for long hours.

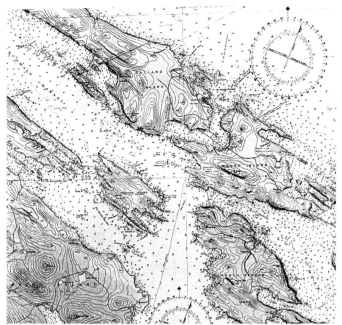

The older charts had drawings of harbour entrances and prominent coastal features. As time went on these were relegated to pilot books. However, before radar was common, topographic features were prominent on charts such as this 1954 chart. It was surveyed from 1902 - 1908 by the R.N.

THE TOOLS

Since the earliest recorded time, mariners have used tools or aids in their quest of distant ports. The "three L's:" log, lead and lookout have been the tools of the coastal navigator for years. The collection of knowledge gained over the centuries and the tools needed for coastal navigation arrived with the early explorers. As is normal with coastal navigation, refinements were made to suite the conditions on this coast.

CHART HISTORY

The charts, we all take for granted, were not as reliable in the early days as they are today. One 19th century navigation book stated: "Instead of considering a coast clear unless it is shown to be foul, the contrary should be assumed." This was, and in some areas, is still good advice.

The history of marine charts dates back to at least 600 B.C. Around 100 A.D., charts were drawn based on a cylindrical projection. This knowledge was lost in Roman times.

Early Mediterranean navigators used directions based on the prevailing winds. They divided these up into eight equally spaced directions. They were called "rhumbs" and were marked on these early charts to aid navigators to steer before the winds. When the compass came into use, the eight rhumb wind rose was painted on the card. This was expanded to 32 points in later years. The rhumb lines were used on charts for years.

The age of exploration created a need for better charts. Toward the end of the 15th century, navigators

were able to obtain latitude by the use of a quadrant and declination tables. Latitudes were put on charts so the navigator could "run down the latitude." Longitude was not on many charts as the navigator had no way of calculating it at sea. The universally accepted prime meridian was not established at Greenwich until 1884. Before this, each country used their own zero longitude. The fathom (6ft. 1.83m.) also differed from country to country.

The Dutch were the first of the northern countries to produce charts. Mercator devised his chart projections in 1569 but it was not in general use for another hundred years. Even then this type of chart we are all familiar with was used only for large-scale ocean charts.

The early 19th century chart, while quite different from a modern chart, was starting to take on the characteristics of the modern chart. By 1800 most of the world had been discovered and charted to some degree. Rhumb lines were being replaced by a modern compass rose.

The first charts a 19th century navigator could have used might have been printed by a government or private business. The charts were put together in atlases covering a large area. They were expensive. Many ships would not have the latest versions even if they were in a port where they were available. Many of them were plane charts rather than the Mercator chart.

One of the most famous privately produced charts in the English speaking world was the "Blue back." The name was taken from the blue-coloured paper used as a backing to protect the chart from rough handling. As early charts were produced in atlases or long rolls, they all were backed with linen, light canvas or layers of heavy paper. These rolled charts were long - some over 6ft.(1.8m.). To save the number of charts required by a ship, small-scale charts and harbour plans were shown as insets. Drawings of headlands and other distinguishing features that would aid the navigator in identifying parts of the coast were also

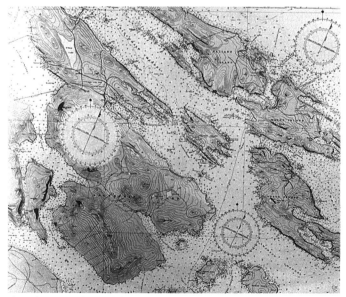

Another section of the chart above. The chart still was not coloured. The soundings are in fathoms (6 feet). While all the topographical information is on modern charts, it is not as prominent. The colour on the modern charts make them easier to read. In Canadian waters the soundings are in meters.

included. Tidal information, soundings and aids to navigation were shown.

The first of these charts was produced by the Englishman, William Heather. He started his business in 1765. Others, including J.W. Norie, carried on the business. They would be used on merchant ships all through the 19th century.

The official charts put out by the United States, the British Admiralty and Canada eventually became the only charts used by mariners in North America. The charts evolved into the type of chart every mariner is accustomed to today. Charts began to have more and closer soundings, subdivided latitude and longitude borders and simpler compass roses. Some charts had magnetic and true roses. The old rhumb lines disappeared. The size of the charts also became more practical.

When electronic navigation became widely used, information such as loran LOP's were printed on the charts. As loran is now discontinued, there will be more changes.

The U.S. Hydrographic and the U.S Coast and Geodetic Survey were noted for their technical innovations by the middle of the 19th century. All chart makers used information obtained from many sources.

The Spanish were first in surveying the coast. Captain Cook did some work on his voyages up the coast. The west coast of North America was first seriously charted in 1792, by Captain George Vancouver. He incorporated information on his charts gained by Spanish surveyors. He showed the lower Columbia River, the coast to Cape Flattery, the southern side of Juan de Fuca, Port Discovery, Puget Sound, and the mainland side of the coast in much detail. Most of Vancouver Island was done with less detail.

Private surveys were started around 1800 by the H.B.C. and other companies of the southern B.C. coast. The Admiralty started surveys in 1846 of Victoria, Esquimalt, Juan de Fuca and other coastal areas. In 1862, the Beaver was chartered by the Royal Navy for survey work on the inside passage. Previously, they had been surveying the coast with the sailing ships H.M.S. Hecate and H.M.S. Plumper.

In the 1850s the U.S. started surveying the west coast. Canadian surveys on the west coast started in 1890 for use in Admiralty charts. The first all-Canadian chart was of Prince Rupert some years later.

Despite this work, there were a lot of uncharted rocks to trap the mariner. In 1884, the Umatilla hit an uncharted reef off Cape Alava. This reef was later marked by the Umatilla light ship.

The northern runs to Alaska claimed a number of ships on uncharted rocks and quite a few charted ones as well. Drag surveying started in WW1. In the 1990s they are still working on parts of the B.C. and Alaskan coasts.

SURVEYING IN THE EARLY DAYS

The early surveys were often not as accurate as they are today. In an 1871 book on U.S. naval surveying, they warn the mariner to be wary of using compass cross-bearings only to fix a position. While at this time major areas of eastern North America were fairly reliable, a lot of the other parts of the globe were not. A lot of the earliest surveys were done with running surveys to give an outline of the coast and some depths. The verification of these surveys took some time to complete.

Due to the limitations of the equipment available to him, even Captain Vancouver made some errors in longitude. It seems he was about ten nautical miles out at Port Discovery and an 8'30" of longitude at Nootka.

RUNNING SURVEY

This can be accomplished as simply as determining the geographical position of the principal points along the coast by means of astronomical observations alone. Due to the inaccuracies of celestial navigation at sea, this is not very reliable. But if true bearings are taken of the points and triangulated with the astronomical data, a greater accuracy can be achieved. This can be taken one step further by running some soundings. The system depends on a combination of astronomical observations and the accuracy of the azmith compass.

Until comparatively recent times, soundings in inshore areas were dependent on the hand-lead line. Small boats used for sounding were propelled by oars. A flying survey of a small area could be done under sail. To obtain distances a common (chip) log was used. If equipped, she could have used two patent logs. Anchored buoys were often used to establish positions. Again, this was not the most accurate method but would help until an accurate survey could be done.

Inland waters were easier to do as you could get ashore to set up markers (signs) and run proper base lines. When a complete survey was properly done, it was very accurate for the time. It was not until modern electronic methods were used that charts started to become very accurate.

In addition to mapping the shore line and recording depths, a topographical survey had to be done. It was very important that a vessel arriving on the coast or entering a harbour should be able to identify land marks by their outline.

Today, charts of most parts of the coast are very accurate. Modern electronic-positioning methods including GPS have greatly increased the accuracy of the surveys. Today, the soundings are closer together. This means there is less likelihood of a towline getting hung up on an uncharted pinnacle. Computers have replaced a lot of the hand work that went into making the charts.

What do you jokers think of my new recipe?

Fisgard Light, built in 1860 from material imported from Britain. The first light on the B.C. coast. Later in the same year Race Rocks light was lit for the first time.

Range lights such as in Sooke guide the mariner past underwater hazards - a rock in this case.

Vessels can have charts on a cd so they can easily monitor them and if connected to a positioning system, show where the vessel is at all times. There are a number of these systems on the market and, as with most things, some are better than others. They do not replace paper charts or the requirement to carry them.

Charts must be kept up to date. It is the responsibility of the crew to update them from the Coast Guard Notices to Mariners.

AIDS TO NAVIGATION - EARLY HISTORY

Where and when the first man put up something or lit a fire to guide him into a harbour is lost in the mists of antiquity. As the city states emerged and sea travel increased, so did rudimentary aids to navigation. Lighthouses were built as far back as 1000 B.C. As they were not very bright, they gave limited help to the mariner. One of the first recorded lights was the tower on Pharos around 300 B.C. It was supposed to have been around 500 feet high and the fires reportedly could be seen for 30 miles.

Harbour lights for guiding mariners past a number of hazards became common. Building a lighthouse that could be seen in the distance and withstand the sea took some time.

Building a lighthouse to withstand the force of the sea was not an easy task. The Eddystone light, some 14 miles off the English port of Plymouth erected in 1779, was one of the first built to withstand the force of the open sea. This was accomplished after several attempts to locate wooden buildings there.

The first lighthouse built in the Americas was one in the late 16th century in Vera Cruz, Mexico. The first North American light was built in Boston, in 1716, followed by a French one on Cape Breton, in 1733.

Most of these early lighthouses had one thing in common: the fires blew out in bad weather and were dim at the best of times. Tallow candles were used in an attempt to overcome the problems of wood and coal fires. Wreckers lit lights along the coast to lure ships to their death so they could plunder their cargo.

In Britain, William Hutchinson, in 1763, used a reflector to gather the light beams and direct them to sea. But it was not until the start of the 19th century that an efficient light was developed.

LIGHTS ON THE WEST COAST

At first, there were no governmental aids to navigation on the coast. To aid vessels getting into harbours and through passes, private marks were set up. This could be as simple as a white mark on a rock. White marks painted on rocks are still used in special areas. Often two lights are put up to form range lights in areas that do not conflict with approved aids.

The need for aids became evident as coastal traffic increased. Accidents increased as vessels tried to find their way into harbours. The need for lighthouses and light ships became indicated after some terrible tragedies. It was very difficult to build lighthouses on most parts of the rugged coast and eastern governments did not think it was worth the money.

In 1860, Fisgard Light at the entrance to Esquimalt Harbour was the first lighthouse on the B.C. coast. That same year, Race Rocks light started operation. The Valencia disaster sped up the construction of Pachena Point.

In addition to major lights, small lights and day markers were established along the coast. Even when searchlights were introduced, it was hard to pick up a white day marker even on a reasonably good night. In the more northern inlets snow would often cover them.

With modern navigational systems and advances in communication, aids to navigation have changed. Most buoys have radar reflectors. Solar panels charge batteries and a lot of lighthouses are automated. The major lights along the outer coast of British Columbia will probably keep some staff. The lights along the U.S. coast are all automated.

Lighthouses were built along the west coast of the U.S. as marine traffic increased. The light on Cape Disappointment, at the mouth of the Columbia, was built in 1856. The first lighthouse in Alaska was built in 1902.

THE COMPASS - EARLY HISTORY

In ancient times, seamen procured their direction from the wind and sea as well as the stars. The wind rose in the Mediterranean traditionally consisted of eight winds. Tramontana (N), Greco (NE), Levante (E), Syroco (SE), Mezzodi (S), Garbino (SW), Ponente (W), and Maestro (NW) were in use long before the compass. Even in modern times, I had to learn to steer by the wind and sea on a fish boat. When the compass card came into use the eight winds were divided up into thirty-two points. Later, each point was quartered.

The instrument seamen most depend on, whether deep sea or coastal, is the compass. The first ones were very crude. The exact dates of the development of the compass are shrouded in the fog of history. They were an iron needle floated on a basin of water. The needle had to be magnetized with a lodestone. While this procedure seems to have been used in the 15th century, some needles were mounted on a pivot as early as 1200. The needle still had to be stroked or "touched" by the lodestone. Sometime in the 13th century the needle was mounted under a card with a painting of a wind rose on it. The compass was mounted in a box and placed on a shelf. The needle could be refreshed with the lodestone from underneath. In medieval times some of the compasses were 4 or 5 inches in diameter. There were often two compasses in wood or brass boxes with a candle placed between them. The housing was called a bittacle. This was the forerunner of the modern binnacle. It seems that around 1500 the compass was mounted in gimbals. The magnetized steel bars mounted under the card arrived in the 18th century. Compasses were still fairly crude until that time.

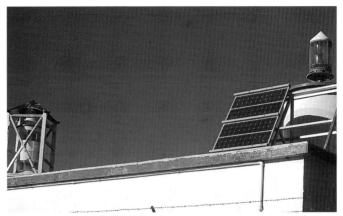

The automated lights are kept operating by using solar panels.

Dispatch! There is no sign of the agent or the custom's officer. Better tell them to hurry up.

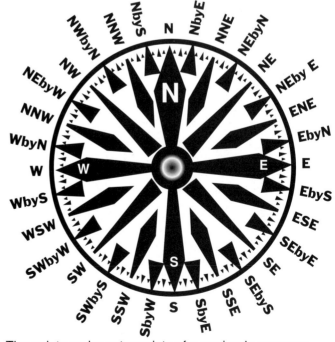

The points and quarter points of a mariner's compass. This card was used until the 360° card took over. It was easy to steer by in poor light.

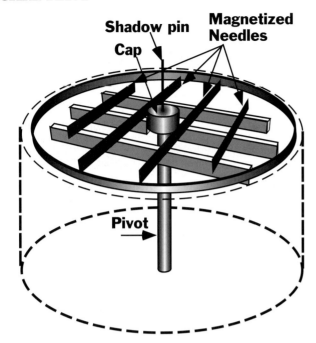

Shadow pin
Cap
Magnetized Needles
Pivot

Above: The dry compass.
Below: Needle.

North South line of compass card

S
Needle
Axis of needle
N
Magnetic axis

THE MODERN COMPASS

In 1768, (Captain Cook's time) variation (difference between true north and magnetic north at the position of the ship) was understood. The compass, while sluggish, was a great improvement over earlier kinds.

With the introduction of large masses of iron machinery a new problem arrived for the navigator. This was the compass error created by the magnetic fields of the metal, known as deviation.

Wooden sailing ships did not have much of a problem with deviation. When the iron hulls were introduced to sailing ships, deviation became a problem as well. Steamships, with their scheduled runs, had more need of an accurate compass than the sailing ship that tacked back and forth across the ocean.

A number of misconceptions abounded. Some thought the compass was affected by fog, strong winds blowing in one direction, the Aurora Borealis, magnetic hills, shoals and thunderstorms. Although these were proven wrong, some of the opinions were expressed in this century. They also tried to shield the compass from the ship's magnetism. Of course, if you were successful in this, the compass would not work.

For years, there was not too much known about deviation and how to correct for it. This was one of the factors in slowing down the development of iron hulls. In 1801-02, Captain Matthew Flinders, R.N., while on a voyage to Australia discovered the use of a vertical, soft, iron bar reduced the effect of induced magnetism in soft iron. In 1838, Sir George B. Airy, started experimenting with the effect of iron hulls on the compass. In 1839 and 1855, he produced papers showing how deviation could be corrected by the use of magnets. The problems of deviation on ships are very complicated. Chapters are written on this subject in many navigational books. I hope professional mariners will forgive me for the following brief description.

When correcting the compass, the ship is put on different headings and the error is noted. Small magnets are placed around the compass to correct this error as much as

Compass card
Float
Bundles of magnetized steel wires encased in brass
Pivot
Communication holes to expansion chamber
Filled with Fluid
Lead weight diaphragm or expansion chamber

The liquid compass. This was the most common type of compass used on tugs for years. A newer style with a built in shadow pin replaced it. To get a bearing the navigator could lay a parallel rule on edge and sight across it. This was not as accurate as an azimuth mirror but was good when there was no other way of getting a bearing.

possible. The ship is then put on another heading and corrections are made again. When the error has been corrected as much as possible the ship is again put on different headings and the remaining error noted. A deviation card is made up from this to be displayed in the wheelhouse or chart room. This procedure is known as "swinging the ship." Soft iron balls often painted red and green, are located on either side of the compass to compensate for horizontal magnetism. A Flinders bar is located on the side of the binnacle for vertical magnetism. Most of the magnets are located in the binnacle. Tugs and other small vessels will have them nailed around the compass.

In the earlier part of the 19th century, they frequently used large 18 or 20 inch compasses with long needles. These compasses were often sluggish. It was common to find a piece of marline attached to the compass bowl so the man at the wheel could give it a jerk to keep it alive, or "keeping the compass afloat." It was found that smaller needles acted faster and if there was a light brass or aluminium ring around the outside, it was steadier. It was also easier to correct for deviation using small needles.

Lord Kelvin was a leader in this research. He produced the first reliable admiralty compass. This was a dry compass using a light card with an aluminium ring around its rim to dampen its movement.

Later on, the liquid compass was introduced. The card was immersed in liquid with a flotation system on the card. The card was heavy enough to stay on its pivot. For many years the liquid was 45 per cent ethyl alcohol (non-drinkable) and distilled water. This was replaced by petroleum distillate in modern compasses.

On all ships, a standard compass was located where the ship's magnetism was least. This usually was on top of the wheelhouse (monkey's island). A steering compass was located at steering station. At times, additional compasses were located in places where deviation would be low. All navigation is done using the standard compass when available. Tugs and small coasters usually did not have the luxury of a standard compass.

At sea the compass could be checked with azimuths (bearings) of the sun and stars. Coastal vessels can check the compass by using ranges of known objects. This has an advantage of working when the heavenly bodies are obscured by low cloud.

If it is properly installed and maintained, the magnetic compass is a reliable instrument. But even in modern times, compasses are often located in poor locations. One tug had the compass mounted on the top of the wheelhouse at deck level. A periscope-type device went down into the wheelhouse for steering. When the vessel rolled, the compass card was all over the place making it useless.

It takes a young seaman some time to learn to steer by the compass. The mate will have a few non-complimentary words to say if he starts letting the ship's head swing more than a couple of degrees. Some years ago a young seaman was put on the wheel of the Union Ship's vessel, "Catala," in Seymour Narrows. He had not been on a vessel with steam steering and gave it a bit too much wheel. The slow steam gear did not let him correct this error and the ship veered off course. After things got back under control, the mate told him to get out of the wheelhouse and not come back until he had learned to steer.

Liquid compass found on most tugs until the 1960s. Photo by *Sheret Courtesy Portland Maritime Museum.*

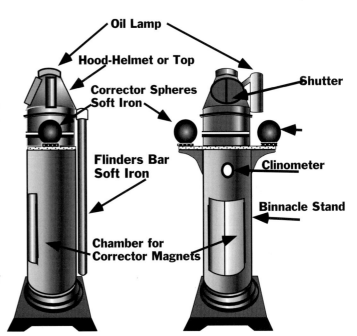

Compass Binnacle

Type of binnacle that would be found on large tugs and ships.

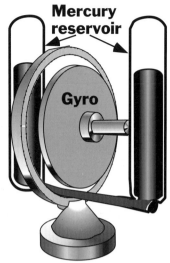

Gyro-compass. Found on medium and large tugs today.

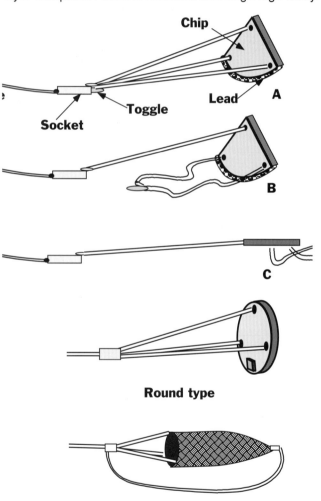

Round type

Bag type

The common or chip log.
A - The log as it was run out.
B - A snap of the line and end pulled out of the toggle.
C - The log flattened out for retrieving.
The round type and the drogue type log.
This log would have been used in the 19th and early 20th century. Tugs would only use logs on long open-water tows.

At one time, every seaman had to be able to "box the compass." That is, recite all the quarter points going in either direction and what the opposite (180°) point was. Now the 360 degree card is in use so this is a lost practise. Today, you are not supposed to use "port" and "starboard" in helm orders so the man on the wheel will understand you. In my opinion, any seaman that is not more familiar with port and starboard than left and right should look for a shore job. Today auto-pilots are used a lot, so a young seaman does not learn to steer and get the feel of his vessel as in earlier times.

THE GYRO-COMPASS

Despite many efforts to overcome the effect of iron ships on magnetic compasses, it soon became apparent that something else was needed. Ships that had been tied up for long periods of time and those that had major work done on them, experienced changes in their magnetic fields. This, along with many other variables, created problems that were hard to eliminate entirely.

While the principle of the gyro was known for some time, it was not until an American, Elmer A. Sperry, and a German, Anschutz-Kampfe, independently invented the gyro-compass that these problems could be eliminated. The first successful test in the U.S. was in 1911.

They soon became standard equipment on large ships. The use of repeaters came later. These were all large machines. They took up a lot of space and took a long time to settle down after they were started. They also needed a reliable and stable source of electricity. For this reason, most tugs and smaller vessels did not use them for years. Eventually, in the late 1960s, smaller ones made their appearance on these vessels.

The magnetic compass does not perform well in the polar regions. The gyro works quite well in this area. While the navigator using a gyro does not have to make corrections for variation and deviation, he will have to correct for latitude and vessel speed. There are other small errors that can occur; however, the errors apply to all headings.

The total theory of the compass is beyond the scope of this book but the principle is, if you have a universally-mounted wheel turning at a high speed, the axis will point in the same direction regardless of how the instrument is held. In order to make it work as a compass, a weight is added to make the axis horizontal to the earth's surface. The pull of gravity and the rotation of the earth will cause the compass to aim to true north. This effect is called precession. The weight usually consists of two mercury-filled reservoirs connected by a tube.

Most of the modern coastal and off-shore tugs have gyros. Small harbour, river tugs and some log boats will still rely on the magnetic compass. As with any mechanical device they can break down, so magnetic compasses are on all vessels.

LOGS

The log is the instrument navigators use to estimate their speed. The first ones were known as Dutchman's log. A piece of wood was thrown over the side and the speed was estimated by the amount of time it took to go the length of the ship. The common log was used for hundreds of years. In the late 19th century, the patent log was perfected.

The common, or chip log, went through stages of evolution. In the 19th century it consisted of a flat piece of wood weighted on one edge. Some of these were circular in shape, triangular or a conical bag.

The chip or, in some cases, a bag, had three short lines from the corners to a toggle. This made the board stand upright in the water and act like a fixed point in the water. When in use, the toggle was jammed into a wooden or bone socket on the end of the log line. The log line had a "stray line" usually around 12 to 15 fathoms in order to let the log clear the wake. This was often marked with a white cloth. If the 28-second glass was used, the line would have markers of cord placed between the strands every 46 feet 6 inches. These markers had knots tied in them for purposes of counting. Hence the term, knots, when describing the speed of a vessel. There were a variety of markers used on these logs over the years but the principle was the same.

The log line was stored on a reel so it could run out freely. After the log was clear of the wake, a man turned over the sand glass. At the end of the interval, the number of knots on the line were counted and that was the speed of the vessel at that time. A short glass of 14 seconds or a normal glass of 28 seconds could be used. In most cases three men were needed for this procedure - one for the reel, one for the glass and an officer to tend the line. There was often a tripping line to flatten the log for hauling back. Some mariners did not have much faith in the new patent logs so these logs where still in use before WW1.

Heaving the common chip log. One man held the spool of line while the man at the rail controlled it. The officer timed it with an hour glass.
This operation was not too practical for coastal tugs.

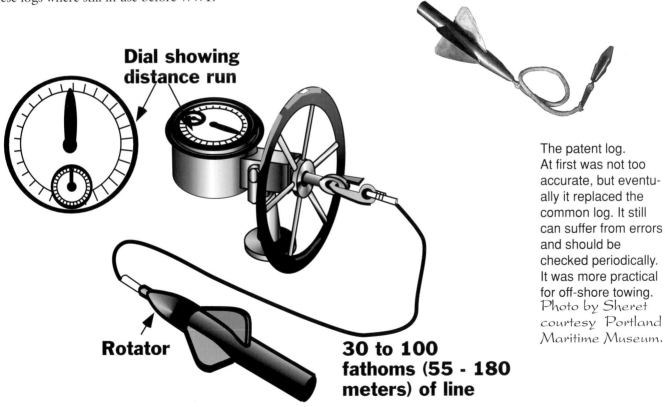

Dial showing distance run

Rotator

30 to 100 fathoms (55 - 180 meters) of line

The patent log. At first was not too accurate, but eventually it replaced the common log. It still can suffer from errors and should be checked periodically. It was more practical for off-shore towing. Photo by Sheret courtesy Portland Maritime Museum.

PATENT LOG

The patent log was invented to overcome the shortcomings of the chip log. The first attempts were made in the 17th and 18th centuries but they were unsuccessful. In 1802, Edward Massey invented one with a streamlined rotator with the dials connected to it. You had to haul the whole thing inboard to take a reading. This was a very popular instrument in the 19th century. In 1861, Thomas Walker patented the Harpoon log and, in 1884, he patented the Cherub log where the dials could be read on board without hauling. In the 20th century several logs attached to the bottom of the hull were used, known as bottom logs.

Logs were not too useful on coastal tugs as the wheel wash and towline caused problems. On long off-shore tows they were used in accordance with any other ship.

LEAD LINE

The lead line, in one form or another, was one of the earliest tools used by the mariner. The earliest method was probably shoving a long stick over the side of the canoe to find a bottom. An unmarked weighted line was the next advancement. The leadsman would measure the line by stretching it between his outstretched arms - about six feet on the average man. This is from where the fathom measurement derived.

Eventually, a lead line with standard markings evolved. This was known as the hand-lead line. The markings were designed to be felt as much as seen. The usual markings were as follows:
2 fathoms a leather with two tails
3 fathoms a leather with three tails
5 fathoms white rag (canvas)
7 fathoms red rag (bunting)
10 fathoms leather with a hole in it
13 fathoms blue rag (cloth)
15 fathoms white rag
17 fathoms red rag
20 fathoms cord with two knots.
For deeper water a deep-sea lead was used. The markings for it were:
first 20 fathoms same as the hand lead;
for each additional 10 fathoms add one knot to the cord;
on each 5 fathoms use a cord with one knot or a piece of leather.

On larger vessels, sounding machines were installed but most tugs only had the common lead line. When electronics were introduced the echo sounder was used. At first it was quite crude, but you could easily follow a drop-off with it in poor visibility.

Now, every tug has an echo sounder. As tugs often work in shallow water, it is well used.

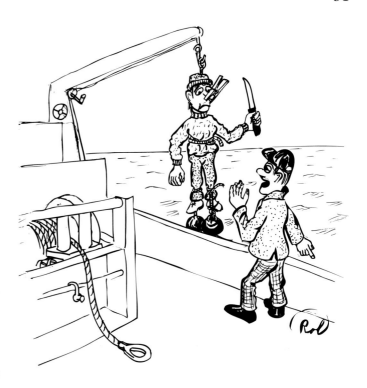

All you have to do is cut the line out of the wheel when we lower you down.

CHRISTMAS

On the B.C. coastal tugs, Christmas has always been the one time of year when the crews could be sure of being home. The boats are in their home port for at least three days. Even when days off were unheard of, the tugs all headed home for the season. A log tow might wind up with half a dozen extra boats on it to ensure arrival in a safe tieup before Christmas eve. Owners marvelled that tugs and tows made better time than they had all year.

There is always a big rush at midnight on Boxing Day to get the vessels to sea again. Just after midnight, all the crews start moving tons of stores down to the tugs. Dispatch tries to organize all the orders and last minute repairs are done as engines are warmed up. As the tugs depart, the skippers all hope their tows are not buried under five or six other barges. At one time, all the tugs had a Christmas tree on their masthead. Some years ago, a tug was standing by an oil barge in a upcoast camp. The seaman decided to go in the woods to get a tree for the mast. When it started to get dark and there was no sign of the man, the crew started a search. They found the lost deck hand and a small tree with most of the branches missing.

New Years is just another working day on most tugs. On one old steamboat, they blew the whistle at midnight and threw last year's tide book over the side.

On the U.S. tugs, time off at Christmas depends on the company, union and where the vessel is operating. The crews on the longer runs do not get time off at this time of year unless the vessels happen to be in port.

3
WORKING WITH SHIPS

Four tugs pushing the bow of a loaded bulk carrier around. The large ships that come in to Roberts Bank coal port need a lot of power to move them just as the tankers do in the American ports a little further south. With the new, powerful, tractor tugs you probably would not see that many tugs pushing in one place.

An American tug assisting a ship. The tug has lines up to the ship so she can keep in position and push or back on the ship. Below: The Canadian tug has no lines on the ship. She is pushing the ship's bow around as it backs up.

SHIP HANDLING

Working with foreign-going ships has always been a major part of the work for tugs worldwide. On the west coast, sailing ships frequently had to be towed for miles from the open ocean to the various ports along the inner coast. When big steamships started arriving they needed assistance while docking. This need increased as the ships got larger and larger. The type and size of the tugs changed as the ships changed.

The average size of foreign-going sailing ships in 1885 was 365 tons. Some ships would have been bigger but not too many were over 2,000 tons even in the later part of the 19th century. Some sailing ships of over 5,000 tons displacement were built in the early part of the 20th century.

The early steamships visiting coastal ports were small in comparison to the ocean-going ships of today. In the 1880s they were not much bigger than sailing ships, around 1,300 gross tons. The Liberty Ships of WW11 were 7,000 gross tons, 10,800 displacement tons. Other ships of the time would be smaller. A tanker would be around 15,000 deadweight tons. In ports without too much current, these vessels could dock with the aid of a boat to run their lines ashore if there was not much wind.

In many situations, they still needed tugs to assist them. In the early fifties, the average tanker was around 20,000 deadweight tons. This rose to 30,000 tons by the sixties. Tankers and bulk carriers of 250,000 tons were built in the eighties. Other types of ships were built in the

Forest Prince under tow. The tugs worked with sailing ships for years. Some of them wound up as barges.
B.C. Archives

Most ships today are so large that it takes several tugs to assist them to dock.

30,000 to 50,000 ton range. As the ships got larger, nearly all of them needed a tug or tugs for docking.

Ships arrive or depart at any time, day or night. It is very costly for the ship owner if there is any delay in arrival or departure times. The tugs must be there when called. However, the ship can arrive late or she may not finish loading on time. When this happens the tugs must standby until needed. This can create a major headache for dispatch. In some areas weather can delay the operation as well. Weather is often quite critical when bringing a large ship into a dry-dock as there is little room to manoeuvre.

Tugs in the area of docking ships are usually working with a "live vessel," that is, the ship can use her own propellers and rudders. The pilot on the ship uses the tugs in assisting him with manoeuvring. If going into a place were the ship can not use her own power, or the engines are down for some reason, the tugs must be powerful enough to move the ship around.

One of the dangers of handling ships on the towline is "getting in irons," or "girding." When a tug is pulling any direction other than the direction the ship is moving, the tug can be rolled over by the heavy ship. Depending on the location of the tow winch, the tug can lose her ability to turn due to the pressure on the towline. The further aft the winch is, the greater the difficulty of getting out of this situation. The towboat captain must know where the danger point is for his tug. This is a judgement call as there are many factors to consider: the speed of the ship, the amount of wind, the type of towing gear and the ability to release it if necessary. If the pilot or docking master knows the capabilities of a particular tug, he will not get it into trouble. The towboat skipper must make the final judgement. He must not be too cautious as the safety of the ship is extremely important. There have been a few tugs rolled over from this with loss of life. There is always a man standing by the release in case of necessity. In some parts of the world, special release hooks, known as tow hooks, were used when towing ships. On modern tugs, electric releases are installed. Unfortunately, if the skipper waits too long, the towline can jam on the drum and it will not release. With these releases, if there is time, the tug can run line to get out of trouble then shorten up to regain control of the ship.

When a small harbour tug finished pulling a ship out of the dry-dock, they kept the towline on so she could help steer the ship until it cleared the harbour. The ship had the tug pull the stern over. When the tug was pulling at nearly right angles, the ship started her engines. The tug could not get around and was starting to go over. The tug let her nylon towline go. The ship was gaining speed all the time. When she passed the tug she picked up the towline in her propeller. The tug then had to let the whole line go or be towed under. The ship was last seen heading for sea with hundreds of feet of heavy nylon towline wrapped in the propeller.

There is quite a different approach to docking procedures between American and Canadian tugs. Canadian tugs often are not made fast to the ship while American tugs usually are.

American-docking tugs usually make fast to the ship. There are a number of ways this is done depending on the type of ship and the conditions that are likely to be encountered. Usually, at least one tug is made fast to each end of the ship. They will use a bow line and a backing line. This lets the tug turn perpendicular to the ship when necessary, or pull back slowing the ship down. Some tugs are equipped with a light line running from the towing winch through a block near the stern and up to the ship. The towboat can pull herself perpendicular to the ship. In this position, she can push the ship toward the dock or pull it off as needed. A towline, from additional tugs, may be put up on the bow or stern so the tugs can totally control the ship. As with all ship docking, there can be problems. If the ship is going too fast, the tug may not be able to hold her stern out with her lines. If something goes wrong and the tug gets wrapped around the bow, she could be in danger of tipping.

The new tractor or Z-drive tugs (steerable rudder-propellers) have changed the way this is done on both sides of the border. The tug can supply power in any direction. The tug is not likely to "get in irons" because it can turn in any direction. There is a winch forward, so a heavy line can be sent up to the ship through a fairlead on the bow. The tug is held in position by the line and can pull off with almost as much power as she can push. They can easily manoeuvre on a towline so they can pull in nearly any direction. On large ships, other tugs are often still needed to handle the weight.

Canadian west coast conventional tugs usually only use lines on ships when they are towing them. With tugs connected by towline to each end of a ship, the ship can be manoeuvred nicely. The stern tug or tugs are towed backward so the ship must not get too much headway on. The ship does not use her engines when this procedure is used.

For most docking jobs, the tugs push on the side of the ship as required by the pilot. To be effective, the ship must be going slow enough for the tug to get her stern out when pushing. The tugs can be moved around the ship to where the most power is needed. Usually, tugs are placed on both sides of the ship. The ones closest to the dock have to get out of there at the last moment before the heavy ship crushes them against the dock. This can be entertaining, especially when there are other tugs trying to do the same thing.

On smaller ships using only one tug, it will go from one end of the ship to the other as needed. When docking large bulk carriers many tugs are used. As most of these tugs are designed for general towing, some problems can arise getting all the tugs in the right place alongside a moving ship. A few masts have disappeared and some housework crumbled in the process. If there is much wind, the small tugs will bang around the ship in the sea.

Smaller tugs will often take lines from the ship to mooring buoys. A deck hand must get on the buoy in order to make the lines fast to the mooring hooks. The task of "buoy-jumping" in bad weather is for the young and agile. Docking ships is very seldom boring.

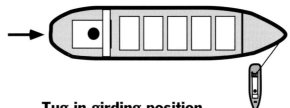

Tug starts to pull bow of ship around.

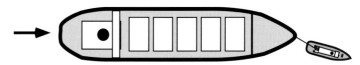

Tug in girding position.
Must let go towline or roll over.

Tug in girding (tipping) position. If the tug pulls too far over, the ship will pass her. If she can't release her line in time, she will roll over and sink. On the east coast and in Europe they had towing hooks with a quick release to avoid this.

A nylon towline as used on this harbour tug can be let go or cut much easier than a wire line.

Above: Cates tug with towline up in Vancouver.
Left: Towing a ferry through Johnson Street bridge. The two tugs line her up with the hole before going through.

A dead ship (one without its own power) is towed into Esquimalt Harbour by an American tug, owned by Crowley Marine Services "Red Stack," with the Canadian Seaspan tug on the stern to help steer the ship. Two local tugs have arrived to assist the ship in the Harbour. The Seaspan tug on the stern will stop the ship when it gets near the dock. The other tugs will push the ship alongside and hold it there until it is all fast. The ship and the tugs are under the control of the pilot on the ship.

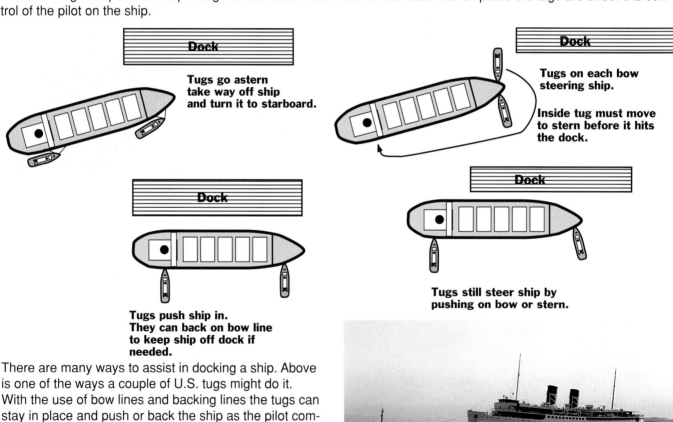

Dock

Tugs go astern
take way off ship
and turn it to starboard.

Dock

Tugs on each bow
steering ship.

Inside tug must move
to stern before it hits
the dock.

Dock

Tugs push ship in.
They can back on bow line
to keep ship off dock if
needed.

Dock

Tugs still steer ship by
pushing on bow or stern.

There are many ways to assist in docking a ship. Above is one of the ways a couple of U.S. tugs might do it. With the use of bow lines and backing lines the tugs can stay in place and push or back the ship as the pilot commands. Larger tugs and crews are needed for this method.

Top right: The way Canadian tugs might dock a ship.

1. With a tug on each bow the ship can be steered into the dock.

2. The inside tug would move around to the stern when the ship is close to the dock. She can push the stern in while the other tug holds the bow. The tugs will hold the ship alongside until she is all fast. The pilot gives all the commands to the tugs as to where he wants them and how hard he wants them to push.

Moving the Princess Marguerite from Esquimalt to Victoria. At times ships are towed without any power of their own. They often do not steer that well so a tail boat is used. The tail boat will swing around and stop up the ship when it approaches the dock.

Tacoma in the 1970s. One tug runs her towline to the bow of the ship while the other Foss tug makes up to the ship. The ship is worked away from the dock and out into the waterway.

The ship is out in the waterway with a tug on each side to steer her.

The ship is assisted all the way to Commencement Bay were the tugs will let go. Today, tractor tugs would probably handle the job in a different manner.

The salt ship, Argyll, is assisted through Second Narrows in Vancouver by a Cates tug. This ship used to deliver salt to Vancouver and Tacoma.

What do ya think Joe. Should I inform the pilot he forgot to let the tug go?

Modern bulk carriers and tankers are very big and heavy. They need a lot of power to move them or stop them. If a ship of this size hits a dock, even at a very slow speed, a lot of damage will be done. This is a loaded one departing Roberts Bank.

Tug No. 1! You can stop pushing now and get out of there.

In small ports called out ports by the pilots, such as Chemainus B.C., small tugs assist ships as they always have.

Modern tractor tugs such as the Seaspan Discovery, 4,000 hp. tug 104 ft. (32 m.) have changed the way ships are assisted. Their ability to apply power in nearly any direction has taken some of the problems out of ship handling. They are used for more than docking. Vessels, such as the Garth Foss, escort loaded tankers coming in from Alaska. The ships are escorted from Port Angeles to the refineries. These tugs are powerful enough to stop a tanker. As they can pull from the bow, they can hook up to the ship in a hurry if needed.

Above: Tugs meet incoming ship to assist with docking. Right: The small, powerful river tugs are good for working around the ships even if tractor tugs are used. If it is blowing and the sea starts to pick up, these tugs bounce around a lot.

4
LOGS & LOG BARGES

Four-wide tow (four booms wide) up short.
The tug shortens up the towline before entering passes and while waiting tide.
The towline is shackled on to a pendant connected to the towing bridles. The bridles are shackled to heavy towing straps. The straps are choked around the sidesticks. In the gulf, they would form a figure of eight rather than a simple choke.

Deck hand packing a chain across a boom. This photo was taken before lifejackets were mandatory. Yarding booms is hard work.

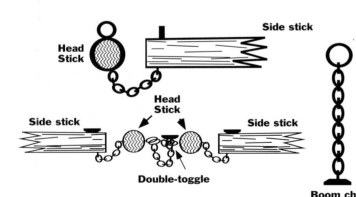

The boom sticks that make up the perimeter of the boom are secured with boom chains.
When booms are coupled together, the coupling chains from one boom are double toggled into the ring of the next boom.

WHERE IT STARTED

With the advent of a permanent population on the west coast of the continent, the need for lumber greatly increased. Wood was also in short supply in parts of Europe. The gold rush and the rapid development of towns and cities in California created a need for good lumber. Lumber mills started springing up all over.

Early steamships were not an economical way of moving bulky material such as lumber. The lumber had to be shipped by sail. Large lumber schooners were used on many of the long coastal runs while the square-rigged ships hauled lumber on the longer runs to Europe.

The compound steam engine became viable in the 1880s. These engines were installed in a few of the schooners, letting mill operators load lumber in the semi-protected bays on the Californian coast. Unlike the protected waters of the north west, the tug and tow concept could not be used in these waters. However, much to the annoyance of the steam schooner crews, some large rafts were towed from the Columbia River to San Francisco.

In the Pacific Northwest and British Columbia, the mountains made road and rail building difficult. The many islands and inlets made the tug and tow concept work. A tug can move a tremendous amount of timber with one vessel and a small crew. The logs could be delivered to the mill without the problems of loading and unloading a ship. While the log tows seem slow moving, more timber could be delivered than could be done with repeated trips of a coastal freighter.

The first tug to tow logs was the famous, Beaver. Most of the first vessels engaged in towing logs were wood-burning paddlewheelers which often doubled as freight and passenger vessels. Sidewheelers and logs do not go well together so when steam engines became available for propeller-driven boats, tugs were soon built for servicing the mills.

Not all of the 19th century boats were big. Small steam tugs working up the coast did a bit of everything. They often towed small groups of logs where they would be made up into a boom. They also would use small scows to move supplies, machinery and the odd cow to camps. As wood was readily available, most of these boats were wood-burners. The owner-operators had to do all their own maintenance, including beaching the boat to paint the bottom. The records are imprecise but most of these boats probably had small, single-cylinder or compound engines.

LOG BOOMS

For many years, one of the main-stays of the tow-boat industry was delivering logs to the mills. Even today, when log barges are used for moving logs over long distances, they have to be boomed up after the barge dumps them. The booms are towed to the mills for use as they are needed. A huge amount of timber can be moved by one tug.

Early mills in Puget Sound and British Columbia had a good supply of logs around the mill. As this timber diminished, the loggers had to go farther afield. At first, the logs were skidded to the water by oxen or horses. Because of the difficulties of skidding large quantities of logs to the water, the booms were relatively small. If the logs could not be moved directly to the mills, they went to the nearest sheltered water and were made into booms for towing.

Later, rail was used to bring the logs to the nearest bay where they could be boomed up. The first rail logging in B.C. started, probably in the 1880s, at Chemainus. In many areas, bigger tows could be assembled in one place. Most of the booms were flats. Despite the increase in machinery used by the companies, hand loggers worked along the beach and operated for years.

The railway era ended in the fifties. By this time, moving the logs by truck had taken over. Now, helicopters are used in some areas. The market changed as well. More pulp mills were being built which changed the type of timber needed and, consequently, the towing industry.

After the logs reach the water, they are made up as individual booms in a booming ground by boom men. The type of boom built, flat or bundle, will depend on the location and whether it is going to be towed or loaded on a barge. The logs are often sorted by species, such as cedar or fir. At one time, the logs might go into a Davis Raft for open-water trips.

The booms are made by chaining boom sticks together around the perimeter to hold the logs. A boom stick is a log approximately 66 feet (20 m.) long with holes drilled in each end to take the chains. At one time, the boom men had to drill these holes by hand but, as with everything else, power took over.

The boom when made up is one stick wide and one or more long. A section is one boom stick long. Eight sections is a common length but the booms can run from one to ten or eleven sections long. With flat booms, if the boom man knows his job, the logs are stowed side by side with the butts aiming the same direction. Larger logs should be placed on the outside of the boom to give the smaller logs some weather protection. To keep the shape of the boom, logs called swifters are pulled up on the logs at each section and chained in. Near each end other logs, called riders, are pulled up and secured. The boom should be tight, but not so stiff that logs will be easily forced out under the side sticks when the boom is towed. On bundle booms where swell is expected, wires are used instead of wooden riders and swifters. In these cases, each log is dogged. That is, bolts are screwed into the logs and made fast to the wires.

The size and buoyancy of the logs vary greatly. Small hemlock logs barely float, while large fir logs float fairly high. Flat booms, made up of short peewee logs, make it more challenging for the people working on them. As each log will not hold a man up, he must move fast from log to log across the boom till he finds a bigger log to work off. If he does not move fast enough, or misses his step, he will wind up in the water. He is usually packing a heavy boom chain and a peavey or some other gear. Skippers tend to get mad if the seamen lose too much gear should they fall in.

Another type of boom is the bundle boom. This boom is made up the same way as the flat boom except the logs are bundled together. A number of logs, often a log-

Right: The crew getting a chain. As the tug pushes the corners of the booms together, the toggle is brought through the ring on the other boom twice to make a "double toggle."

Steam tug, Active, in 1936. The old steam tugs were big and had a large crew. They were hard to manoeuvre so the crew had to do a lot more bull work.
Courtesy "The Museum at Campbell River"

Things did not always go as planned. The City of Lund, was rammed and sunk by a ship, the Admiral Evans, in Duncan Bay, 1920.
Courtesy "The Museum at Campbell River"

The Harken 10, arriving Baynes Sound with a five-wide tow. The newer log boats are smaller and can handle a greater load than the older boats. The crew is much smaller on these diesel boats than the old steam tugs.

A tow going into the locks in the ship canal on the way to Lake Union.

ging truck load, are tied together with wire or bundling straps to make a bundle. The bundle is dumped into the water and stowed in the boom. These booms will usually take more weather than a flat boom and include many more logs in each section. A big bundle will draw about ten feet making them much harder to tow. They are also a steadier platform on which to work.

At first, Davis Rafts were used for moving logs from exposed waters, such as Port Renfrew, but eventually big bundle booms were used. These booms were made up with heavier chains and wires. When towing out of San Juan (Port Renfrew), the big bundle booms were out on the buoys three wide. The crew had to get the extra heavy towing gear on while the booms were moving around in the swell. At times, tugs had to wait days for the swell to recede enough in the straits for the tow. In later years, due to better weather information on the radio, the tug would be employed towing scows around Sooke or Victoria till the swell went down.

When they were towing out of Nitinat Lake, the small boats would often tow the boom over the bar into the ocean. The tug would tow the boom to San Juan to be made up into a bigger tow before going south. As with the Renfrew booms, they would be towed three wide to Becher Bay where they would be put into bigger tows.

At other times, a larger tug would wait off Nitinat till the smaller tugs brought the booms out over the bar. It would then couple the booms together in an ocean swell. When chaining these booms together, the seaman had to get at least a single-toggle hookup when the booms came crashing together in the trough. It was a case of Jack be nimble, Jack be quick or Jack was flattened by the booms coming together.

After the booms are built, they are connected or "yarded" together with chains to make up a tow. All the coupling chains are "double toggled," that is, the toggle is put through the ring on the other chain twice. This pre-

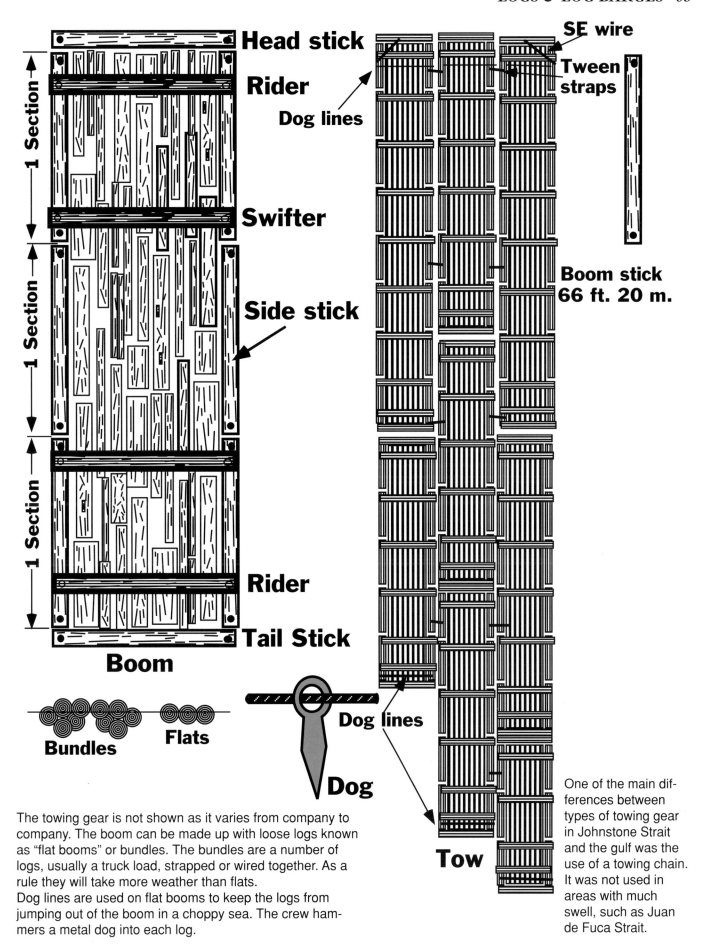

Head stick

Rider

Dog lines

1 Section

Swifter

1 Section

Side stick

1 Section

Rider

Tail Stick

Boom

Bundles

Flats

Dog

Dog lines

SE wire

Tween straps

Boom stick 66 ft. 20 m.

Tow

The towing gear is not shown as it varies from company to company. The boom can be made up with loose logs known as "flat booms" or bundles. The bundles are a number of logs, usually a truck load, strapped or wired together. As a rule they will take more weather than flats.
Dog lines are used on flat booms to keep the logs from jumping out of the boom in a choppy sea. The crew hammers a metal dog into each log.

One of the main differences between types of towing gear in Johnstone Strait and the gulf was the use of a towing chain. It was not used in areas with much swell, such as Juan de Fuca Strait.

Chemainus Towing yarding a tow in Becher Bay. The men on the booms are trying to get a chain across the head end. There used to be a lot of logs stored in the bay. At times several tugs would yard tows simultaneously. Now there are very few stored logs there. The tug is the Hamilton Baily, before it went to the east coast.

A bundle. In most cases they float higher than flats. However, some hemlock pulp bundles are barely floating.

vents the toggles from jumping out in a chop. A tug may pick up booms from a number of booming grounds to make up a tow. The tows are made up with flat booms or bundle booms or a combination.

The boom chain used for making up the booms and connecting booms together to make up a tow, has a ring on one end and a toggle on the other. The old chains used on the west coast and Port Renfrew were heavier and had a smaller ring with a bar across the bottom. These chains, designed to work in swell conditions, were heavy and hard to handle.

The tug or small yarding tugs will make up a tow yarding assorted booms together. When yarding up a tow, the booms are dug out from the other booms in the tieup and chained together. The booms are all numbered for identification when they are built. This operation can take many hours and, in some cases, involve several boats. At one time, it was not unusual to see a number of boats in a bay yarding several tows simultaneously. In areas prone to current and sudden winds, such as Becher Bay near Victoria, the tugs had to be careful not to cut too many booms loose at one time or it was easy to wind up with the whole booming ground adrift.

On one occasion in Becher Bay, while the crews were stopped for lunch, a green mate went out on the booms and let a boom go that was needed for the tow. Unfortunately, he let the whole booming ground go while at it. Needless to say, the afternoon westerly hit with a bang. The rest of the afternoon was spent chasing booms before they hit the beach. The majority of logs had to be towed back to the tieup against the gale by the more powerful boats. The yarding boat would grab one loose boom and pull it away from the beach till it had to let go and rescue another boom. This kept everyone busy for hours. When, at last, everything was under control again, the boats still had to yard the tows together before tide time.

Yarding logs is not a dry job as far as the crew is concerned. You usually have to stick your arm in the water to let the chains go or make them fast. In the winter this can be a bit cool. You can appreciate that, after leaving a warm bunk, the act of breaking a layer of ice with a peavey to get at a chain took some effort. Sooner or later, everyone fell in especially if you were working on flat booms at night. Watching one of the deck crew go for an unscheduled swim usually created some laughter from engineers and the cook.

A tug was yarding up its tow in Port Angeles when a chain had become jammed under a stick. The mate asked the skipper to shove on the side stick with the boat while they tried to clear the chain with a peavey When the boat bumped the stick, it hit the end of the peavey. This, much to the skipper's annoyance, catapulted the peavey and the two guys pulling on it into the water.

Some companies did not yard logs at night for safety reasons. Before regulations were enacted on the number of hours a man could work in a 24-hour period, these yarding operations could go on night and day. It was not unusual for three-man yarding tugs to yard for twelve

Left: Before a tow can depart lanterns are put on each corner so other vessels will see it at night. The tug must stop and fill the lanterns every so often. Now some booms have electric lights operated by battery.

hours straight in Howe Sound, then yard in the North Arm all night and be back out to the Sound for another yarding session by daybreak.

The maximum size of the tow depends on the power of the tug and whether it is going to be towed through narrow passes or open water. A small steam tug might have found 24 sections a good load, while a modern diesel tug would be able to haul a load many times this size. Too much power can pull a tow apart. Modern log boats are often smaller boats with around 800 to 1,200 horse-power in them.

The tug may take all the logs to one place such as the North Arm or it may drop off booms on the way. Depending on market conditions, booms are often bought and sold several times in a few months. It is not unusual for a boom to be sold to another owner while it is being towed.

Before radio, once the tug departed with a tow, there was no way to contact the skipper for a change of orders until he delivered the tow. Later, when phone or telegraph lines were installed, limited communication was practicable. In later years, it was not unusual for a small air-craft with log buyers to land alongside the tow.

Smaller tugs often pick up booms from a variety of booming grounds. These are towed to a larger storage area where the company has foreshore rights. When the towing company gets an order for a number of booms, it dispatch-es a more powerful tug to make up a tow. In Howe Sound, north of Vancouver, there are many of these storage grounds. The river tugs can make up a tow and deliver it to the mills in the Fraser River as they are needed.

Booms are often yarded out of the mainland inlets and islands inside northern Vancouver Island by smaller tugs. This area is known as the "jungles." The larger tugs bring the tows down Johnstone Strait. Over the years, thousands of booms were towed from Johnstone Strait and the many inlets along the mainland coast. Most of these tows proceed down through the Green Point Rapids, Wellbore Rapids and the Yaculta Narrows. This involves working the tidal currents and waiting for slack water in some places. If the tow was going all the way to Howe Sound or the North Arm, it would start working its way down the Strait of Georgia. Tug and tow would probably have to wait for weather in such places as Ragged Islands, Grief Point and Southeast Rock. Today, some of these longer tows have been taken over by the log barge.

Many other tows originated in the gulf (Strait of Georgia). At one time, there were small camps all over the Strait of Georgia and the many Gulf Islands.

The mills on the north coast of British Columbia and southeastern Alaska are kept supplied with the aid of tugs. In some areas, the logs are now picked up by barges but there are still many booms used.

TOWING

The tug that pulls the made up tow may not be the same one that yarded the tow together. After a tow is yard-ed, it must be made ready for towing. A boom plan show-ing where all the booms are stowed must be made by the crew if the yarding tug did not leave one. The boom is

I see Joe hasn't worked on a logtower before.

Mate driving dogs into the logs. They reduce log loss on flat booms by keeping the logs in the boom.

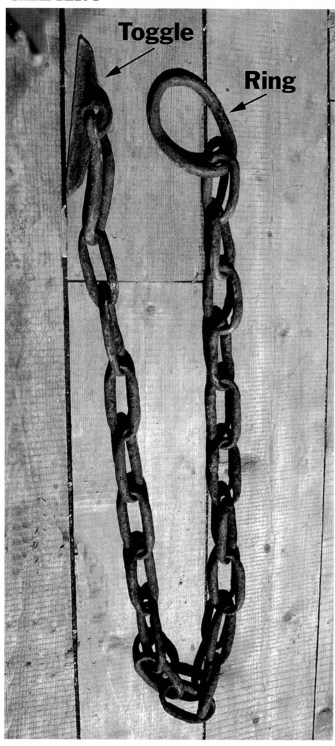

A well worn boom chain. As they get older, rust and wear reduce the size of the links. Old chains, while much easier to pack, are a weak point in the tow. Some camps use old chains when they make up a boom to save money. The crew will take this into account when making judgments on how much weather a tow can take. At times, preventer straps are put in beside weak chains. The crew may not have enough time to do this before they have to depart with a tow to catch a tide.

checked to make sure all the chains are in correctly and there is no apparent damage to any of the sticks. The skipper will assess how much weather the tow will take and how it will handle.

After this, "tween straps" and chains are put in between the rows of booms. Preventer straps may be needed on weak spots. On flat booms, dog lines are often needed. In the gulf, "southeast wires" can be used to save the front corners of the tow. Lanterns are placed on the corners and then the towing gear is put on. Depending on the size of the tow and the type of gear used, this may take several hours.

The type of towing gear the tug uses will depend on the area and the width of the tow. The tugs that operate in Johnstone Strait and the gulf use a different type of towing gear than the ones operating in more open-water conditions such as Juan de Fuca.

Before departing with a tow, the skipper has to assess the weather. In a lot of places, he may have to wait for weather and the right tide. While tows vary in their ability to withstand choppy seas, most of them will break up if a strong wind and sea "make up." Today with radios, the skipper listens to government forecasts and to other boats talking. But before radio, he had to size up the weather solely from his own observations. He still will spend time checking local conditions. You may see a tug drifting round outside a bay watching the weather. As weather is one of the biggest challenges a skipper has, he will be watching and listening for weather signs the whole trip.

The weather and sea conditions can change quickly despite his best estimate. After spending time watching the weather and listening to the forecasts, a skipper departed Renfrew with his tow. Just before he got to San Juan Point, the swell increased dramatically. By the time he got the tow turned around half of it was gone. He called for help to round up the lost logs. Another boat was dispatched and the two tugs picked up all the loose bundles. The swell was over ten feet by this time. The deck hands and mates did a wonderful job getting lines on the bundles in the swell. They often had to jump on the rolling bundle to work a line around it so it could be towed in.

A sudden gale could do serious damage to the best built boom. Even in relatively protected waters, a chain could let go and boom drill would start. If there was a lot of current, it might be hard to get back to the tow for repairs without letting it hit a rock. If that happened, you really had a problem. When towing across the gulf everyone has been caught at one time or another. Many tows have been destroyed off the North Arm while the tug is waiting tide in order to get into the river.

There are many places, such as Southeast Rock that the logtowers try to hang on to till the weather subsides. The trouble with many places is that they are exposed to wind from another direction. If the wind suddenly changes, there is a mad scramble to get away and find another refuge for the tow. Grief Point is noted for this. Tugs often stay just inside Porlier Pass or Gabriola Pass waiting for a break in the weather. Dogfish Bay, just outside Gabriola, is a famous place to wait weather. Unfortunately, you can not leave a big tow there on a falling tide or it will hang up on the rocks. In the gulf, where the current is not too strong, a tow can often be hung off on a tieup wire on the head end while waiting weather. In some areas a tow is made fast to the beach with a line on each end. On a falling tide, you have to keep the tow off the beach as it will hang up and go aground on the rocks.

One "scow boat," a tug that normally towed scows, got a log tow for a change. They took the tow into a bay near Bull Pass, on Lasqueti Island, so a "log boat" could take over. They ran the tieup wires to the outside of the tow as you would with a barge alongside a dock. When the tide dropped, the boom was spread all over the rocks. When the other boat arrived, there were a few uncomplimentary remarks made.

At some tieups, such as Ragged Islands north of Powell River, the tow could be left while you went for stores. In the steamboat days, the tug might run over to Union Bay for coal or go to nearby Lund for stores et cetera. It also gave the skipper a chance to contact the office for any change in orders.

When the tug is held up for weather in a tieup, it gives the crew a chance to check the tow. Depending on the tow and what it has been through, repairs are often necessary. The old skippers often reyarded the tows to make them tow better.

Today, if the tug is held up for weather, it may leave the tow in a safe place and head off to tow scows. The big trick is to finish the scow job before you miss a break in the weather.

The other big concern for logtowers is the current. A tug does not make much time through the water with a large log tow. The crew has to work with the currents. In most areas the tide runs harder further away from the beach, so the tug that is bucking the tide will stay close in to the shore. With a fair tide, it will stay offshore to take the greatest advantage of the current.

Back eddies form behind points and rocks. The tug can often buck along the shore in a back eddy till it comes to a point. The tug may be able to buck around the point if it stays close enough to it. In some places, the tug may have to wait for the tide to change or slacken off before it can move its tow.

Bucking along the beach requires local knowledge and skill on the part of the skipper and the mate. The tide can easily set the boom on a rock or, if it gets too far off shore, it will get into the stronger tide and go backwards. If the tail end of the boom is heading for a rock, the tug can pull the head end toward the beach kicking the tail end out. As the currents are very fickle, this does not always work and the tow wraps around the rock before breaking up. The skipper or mate must keep a constant watch for changes in the current and work the tow accordingly.

The eastern entrance to Juan de Fuca Strait and the upper part of Puget Sound is notorious for strong currents and sudden winds. The logtowers try to work the tides in the islands. Some tows go through Deception Pass between Whidbey and Fidalgo Islands but you can still get your tow broken up by choppy seas inside the islands.

There has been a lot of log towing on the north coast as well. The large tides and violent weather give the towboat crews lots of problems. In the winter, freezing outflow winds can hit without notice. It is not much fun trying to repair a tow when everything is freezing and covered in ice.

When leaving Becher Bay to get the start of the flood at Race Passage, the tug works up the back eddies to

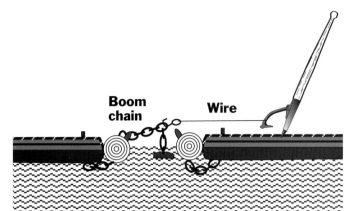

If the tug can not push the booms close enough to "make a chain," a cum-a-long is used. By using the peavey and a wire with a hook on it, the corners can be brought together. With the newer, smaller logtowers this procedure is not used as much as it was with the big steam and early diesel boats.

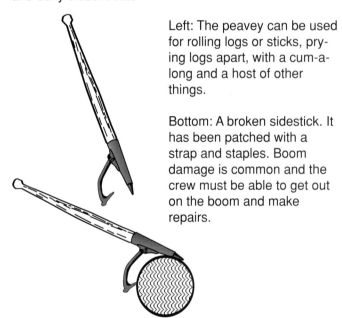

Left: The peavey can be used for rolling logs or sticks, prying logs apart, with a cum-a-long and a host of other things.

Bottom: A broken sidestick. It has been patched with a strap and staples. Boom damage is common and the crew must be able to get out on the boom and make repairs.

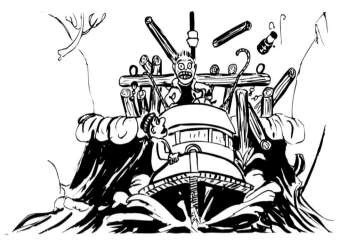

A tad late on the tide, cap?

Bentinck Island. Every once in a while, the current pattern changes and the tow is driven on the rocks. One time when this happened, the tow hit Church Island and promptly broke the inside stick. The tug had to let the tow go before it went aground. It ran back to grab the tail end with a hook line. The boom was peeled off the rock and pulled out into deeper water. The mate and the deck hand were put on the broken tow with a bunch of straps, wires, pike poles and peaveys. The orders were to fix the boom regardless of problems. As the tide was turning to flood, the tug went back to the head end and started towing. The crew on the boom struggled to get the tow held together while the logs were rolling around in the eddies with the tug attempting to pull full speed. At one point, a log got out of the boom with the deck hand on it. It rolled and he was in the water. Fortunately, the mate was able to reach him with a pike pole and got him back to the boom. The tow was patched up well enough to get to Victoria though it was not a pretty looking job. This fact was remarked on by the harbour boat crew in Victoria.

Before entering passes or narrows, logtowers usually have to wait for slack water. Every log-towing skipper has a "black book," a personal notebook of tidal and other information he has collected over the years. It will list how much time the tug and tow will have to leave a tieup before the tide changes to make slack water at a narrows or point. It will also tell him how large a tide he will need.

The tug usually leaves a tieup or starts bucking along the beach in time to make the tide in the narrows. The skipper does not want to arrive too early in the narrows in case the weather comes up.

There is usually a point of no return where the tide will not let the tug and tow turn around and go back. The skipper has to make a decision on the weather before then. Sooner or later, he will get caught and the wind will start popping logs out of the tow or, if his luck has really run out, break it up completely.

TYPICAL TOW

All this necessitates planning. Local knowledge is a must. Every area is different. A typical heavy tow from Becher Bay to the North Arm would take around three

Damaged tow. The tug will pull broken sticks together so the crew can repair them with straps and staples.

Teredos weaken sticks. The holes on the outside are small making it hard to see them on a newer stick.
Right: Picking up loose logs after break up.

The mate getting a single toggle while repairing a boom. If a chain has broken, the crew may have to replace it. Note repair strap beside him.

Above: A tow heading down the gulf (Strait of Georgia) off the sunshine coast. Good weather for log towing.

Left: Small tug delivering a boom to the mill at Comox. The harbour tugs yard individual booms to the mill from the main storage grounds. All booms are numbered. The mill will ask for a boom by its number.

Towing through Enterprise Channel (Trial Is. Pass). The tug has bucked the ebb tide along the beach from Victoria. As the tide starts to slack off, she starts to buck in. She will hit slack water in the Pass. The tide outside Trial Island is still ebbing hard. The tug will buck along the beach until she gets to Ten Mile Point where she will get the start of the flood tide. The flood will take the tug up to Saanichton Spit. She will be safe from any S.E. wind that may come up and she will be in a good position to get the start of the flood off Dock Island near Sidney. By working the tides and the weather, a logtower can make steady progress with his tow.

The tug is pulling full now and starting to make the bend in the channel. There is an underwater reef on his starboard (right) so the skipper must pull well down into the pass before he can start to turn. He must not put too much pressure on the tow when he is turning it or it will break. When he gets past another reef further along, he will turn to port (left) and work along the beach. He will use landmarks to make sure he is in the right position. It is easy to go aground on the many rocks in the area.

At one time, if the weather was bad, many tugs would wait weather in Cadboro Bay. Since all the mills have gone from Victoria, you will never see a scene like this again. In other parts of the coast, logtowers can be found waiting wind and tide.

days. This could be a bit shorter or much longer depending on the size of the tides, the size of the tow and the weather.

The tow would leave Becher Bay about three hours before slack water at the Race. It would take the flood till it got off Victoria. If the weather was still holding, the tug would start bucking along the Victoria waterfront about four hours before low water at Port Townsend. It would buck into Trial Island Pass (Enterprise Channel). The tow would stay tight to the beach at Gonzales Point and work its way through the islands off Oak Bay. The skipper would get the start of the flood off Cadboro Bay. This would take him to Saanichton or Sidney enabling him to get the first of the flood past Dock Island and, hopefully, through Captain Pass. He would then keep on moving up to Porlier Pass.

If the weather was still holding, he would go out through Porlier on the next slack water. He would likely use an assist tug through the Pass if he has a big tow. Around fourteen hours later, he would be off the North Arm waiting for slack water.

Before deciding to go out through the Pass, the skipper must decide if he is going to have enough good weather to get across the gulf. Once out in the gulf his choices are limited. If the westerly starts to pick up before he gets too far out, he can make a run for the Flat Top Islands before the sea starts to damage his tow. When you are only making one to one and a quarter knots, the term "making a run for it" might be stretching it a bit. If he is far enough across, he might be able to get under the Sand Heads if the wind picks up from the southeast. If the westerly comes up, his tow is in trouble unless he can get into Howe Sound. A westerly or a "squamish" (out flow) can hit, creating total disaster while you are waiting tide to get into the North Arm.

There are other ways the skipper could have made this voyage. He might have gone outside Discovery Island if he had a big enough tide. He could have gone through Sansum Narrows instead of Captain Pass or he could have gone out through Gabriola Pass instead of Porlier Pass.

"Tween straps" hanging on a towing winch. They are used to stiffen a boom and to patch a boom if it breaks.

Jordan River

The water is too shallow for the larger tug to come into the river so it anchors offshore. The small river tug goes out to the tug and tows its towline into the boom. After the gear is put on, the boom is let go and the tug begins to pull the boom out. The small tug guides the tail end until it is clear of the bar. The tug will start heading down the coast with the tow.

RIVER TOWING

Yarding in the Fraser River is for the young and the quick. When making up a string to go upriver with the tide, there is no time to waste. Booms are coupled on the fly. The crew must be able to snap a "double toggle" into a ring as the booms come together momentarily. At one time if a deck hand or mate got a chance for a quick nap during the night, he often had to sleep with his clothes and caulk boots on so he could get out on the boom without wasting any time.

Falling in the water in the river is a lot worse than in a normal booming ground as the current can take a man under the boom and drown him. The fresh water is a lot colder than the ocean in the winter time. Working on a tow for hours with wet clothes frozen around you is not considered the best way to spend the night.

When the river is flooding "freshet," the current is even a greater obstacle. When one tug was bringing a string of boom sticks down river, the tug went down one side of the bridge and the sticks down the other. Needless to say, the sticks came loose and had to be retrieved. Two boats got these sticks back under control despite the fact that the current was rolling the sticks around. To do this, the crews had to run along the sticks to get wires around them.

When the tows arrive at the North Arm of the Fraser River, small river tugs often start taking the tow apart. They store the booms in the storage grounds along the river. They start to make up tows for upriver locations. If there is good weather, a number of tows will arrive at the "green light" at low water. There are booms all over the place. The outside tugs will continue towing upriver with the remainder of the tow. Some tugs will drop off their tow without assistance.

The tows for upriver are one wide and quite long. They are yarded up before tide time. When the flood tide starts, they are on their way. There will be one river boat on the head end and one or more boats hooked on to the side of the boom. When the tow gets to one of the many bridges, the boat on the side lets go and assists the tow through the bridge pillar. The highly manoeuvrable river boats can push on the side of the boom till it gets very close to the bridge. One of the less manoeuvrable outside boats tried this and the boom and the tide took it under the bridge removing the mast, stack and the upper control station. This does not mean the river boats do not have their troubles too. Quite a few of them have been sunk in the river. Unfortunately, a number of lives have been lost over the years in the river.

Of course while the logtowers are trying to do their thing, other boats are towing large barges up and down the river. At times, there will be the odd dredge somewhere along the way as well. In freshet season, booms can break away from their tieups. One year, booms started letting go in the upper part of the North Arm ripping out strings of booms on their way down river. There was only one radio band for all tugs in those days so we all could hear the commotion. Every river boat that could be found was busy that night. Point Grey Towing was in charge of damage control. They wound up with logs from assorted booms mixed up together along with pulled up dolphins. It took days to sort out that mess.

Booms are towed down river on the ebb as well. At times, tows will come down from the Hope area. Shallow draft "white water" boats work this area. Tows also go up the main arm of the Fraser River. You have to be able to get from the mouth (Sand Heads) to well above Steveston on one tide or you are in trouble. A powerful outside boat is

When the outside tug gets further upriver, the crews will start stripping the towing gear off the tow. Meanwhile, the river boats are shoving it into the dolphins. The scow boats are trying to get up and down the river at the same time.

At times, one or more tugs will assist the tug and tow. This may be through a pass or up the river. They may be there to apply some more power to the tow so they can "make a tide." If the weather comes up, assist tugs will often try to get the tow to a safe place or repair the booms.

usually on the head end while a number of smaller assist boats push the tow as far upriver as possible.

Of course, the Fraser River is not the only river on which logs are towed. The lower Skeena often has a lot of logtowers.

Logs were a major part of the towing industry in Puget Sound for many years. Logs went back and forth to the mills in Canada and the United States. Southeastern Alaska has boats delivering logs to the mills in various areas. Logs have come from all the inlets in the upper B.C. coast and Skeena River as well. Today, there are certainly not as many logtowers as there once were but it still keeps a lot of people employed.

BEAVER COVE DRYLAND SORT

Beaver Cove, on the north end of Vancouver Island, is a major source of log booms. This has been a major booming ground for years. As with most modern booming grounds, the logs are sorted on land instead of in the water as had been done for years.

Now, logs are brought to the dryland sort by truck or rail. This is one of the few places that rail is still used for log transport. The logs are sorted as to species and size into a form of large rack. When enough logs have been placed in the rack to make up a bundle, straps are secured around it. The bundle is moved to the water. Boom boats shift the bundles into the boom. When enough bundles are stowed

Tow heading upriver at New Westminster on the Fraser River. The tug and tow have just come out of the North Arm. When towing upriver, the booms are made up in a single string (one wide). The tows are quite long.

to complete the boom, it is closed off and riders and swifters are placed to hold the boom together. The finished boom is then towed over to the storage ground.

Tugs with around 2,000 hp. are used to tow the booms south. If the weather holds and they make the tides in the narrows, it will take about seven days to reach Vancouver with a tow.

STEEL STICKS

The shortage of wood has companies experimenting with plastic-coated, steel boom sticks. While a wooden boom stick is 60 to 66 feet (20m.) long, these ones are only 40 feet (12m.) long. They should last five to ten years. The plastic is heavy enough to withstand caulk boots. A rubber coupler with a chain inside is used.

In a June '98 article of the West Coast Mariner, they have figures on what strain a boom stick can withstand. The steel sticks are designed to take 120,000 pound pull. They say a wooden stick can take a 50,000 pound pull. The author's experience has been that all wooden sticks are not created equal when it comes to what strain they can take.

The long tows assisted by other boats. They help steer the tow and keep it from hitting anything such as a bridge.

There are tieups all along the river. Tows are yarded from them and individual booms can be yarded out for delivery to a mill.

Left: Kelsey Bay booming ground in Johnstone Strait. Note white marker on boom showing the boom number.

Canfor's Beaver Cove booming ground. Before the logs are put in the water, they are sorted on the dry land sort. Some years ago most logs were sorted in the water.

They arrive by truck or rail. The logs are first scaled by the B.C. Forest service to determine stumpage and royalty fees. They are moved to the sorting areas to be graded and organized for pulp mills or lumber mills. The sorted logs will then be made up into bundles and dumped into the water. The boom boats move the bundles to the correct boom. After the boom is made up, it will be towed over to the storage ground. The tugs will make up the tows in the storage areas.

LOG SALVAGE

Strapping a bundle.
The sorted logs are placed into these steel containers until they get enough for a bundle. The bundles are strapped so the logs will stay together in the water.

When logs pop out of a boom or there is a major breakup, the loose logs must be retrieved. Each log has a stamp on it so it can be returned to its rightful owner. Some people have the mistaken idea that anything floating loose is theirs by right of salvage. In British Columbia, it is a criminal offence to take loose logs in the water or on the beach. For this reason, licensed log salvagers known as beachcombers do this work. Most of them use fast boats that can quickly get to a tow in trouble.

They patrol the beach looking for stray logs that may have washed ashore. When they get a bunch of logs they will tow them to a designated area. If there is a major log spill, the area is usually closed and only certain boats will be allowed to pick up logs.

This can be a hard way to make a living. Years ago you would see black shapes heading for the tail end of a flat tow. They would bang the tail stick with their boats and get a few logs to pop out under it. The boats were sometimes painted black. The nickname, log pirates, stuck for years. The large bundle booms have made this bit of free enterprise fail.

SAILING DIRECTIONS

For years, skippers and mates have kept their little, black books loaded with useful information. One of the most useful things were directions for getting through holes with log tows. In most cases, a skipper would not go through a pass with a tow if he had not seen it before. The directions helped as a reminder and gave him leaving times.

Departure times were also useful as you knew when to leave in order to be at the pass, etc. for slack water. Little maps also helped.

Do not follow these examples.

The examples below are out of an old book and we can not guarantee their accuracy.

TIDE TIMES FOR LOG TOWS

Sooke - Leave 5 hrs. before LW slack Race Rocks to go to Victoria.

CADBORO BAY

Southbound to Victoria - Leave 2-3 hrs. before HW Port Townsend.

Northbound: Leave 1hr. before LW Port Townsend.

HOLE IN THE WALL

Have 1 1/2-2 hrs. (depending on tide) at Okis Is. Keep along Quadra Is. shore then head for Gypsy Shoal. Go between Gypsy Shoal and Okis Island.

Start towing from Watts Bay 12 hr. before LW. Let boom drift over to Etta Pt. and keep to starboard shore. Then get to port shore. When through hole favour port shore.

Can go right through to Siwasi on one tide depending on load and tide.
Slack water - Seymours - 50 minutes.
Running tide - 1 1/2 hours.

DODD NARROWS

Towing southbound-
1) Hold Joan Pt. very close. Tow sets off hard.
2) Tail boat holds tow close.
3) Tow sets to port.
4) Tow sets to starboard slightly.
Start bucking in 1 hr. before HW slack. Hold to Vancouver Is. shore very close. Have tail boat. Tail sets to port hard if tide is running.

INLAND LOG TOWING

Not all log towing is done on coastal waters. Logs have been towed on the rivers and lakes of the interior for years. At one time, there were river drives where the logs were sent down river in the current. When small tunnel tugs were used on the rivers, they were known as fast water boats. This work required special crews. When the dams were built on the rivers of the upper Columbia watershed,

A bundle on its way to the water. A log stacker has taken the bundle to the ramp where it will slide into the water.

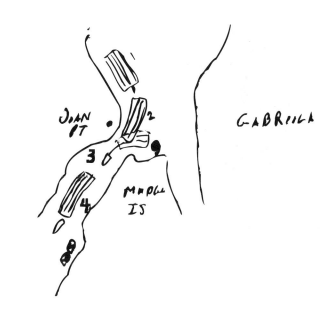

Example in "black book."

Tugs in Castlegar. They use one large tug for towing down the Lake and a number of smaller yarding tugs all over the Arrow Lakes.

The logs come down to the dump by truck near Nakusp. The load is strapped to make a bundle. The bundle is then pushed off the truck and into the water. Similar procedures are used on the coast.

Top: Unlike most coastal operations, the bundles are connected by wires choked and dogged on the logs. A string of bundles forms the perimeter of the booms. Loose bundles are stowed inside.
Bottom: Tug with boom lower end of the Lakes near Castlegar. The boom looks more like a bag boom when it is towed.

there was a lot of activity getting the timber out before the water levels rose. Rivtow sent men and equipment to the area. They worked with the local men to get the job done. Some of the operations in the rivers with the fast water boats were hectic.

Logs booms are still towed on the Arrow Lakes but a lot of the other work has disappeared. At the present time, there is one larger tug and a number of yarding tugs working the area.

Nowadays, the logs are bundled on the trucks before dumping in the water. The booms are not made up in the same way as they are on the coast. The bundles are strung out end to end connected by wires. The string is doubled to form a big pocket. Loose bundles are shoved into the pocket to make a form of bag boom.

A larger tug tows these booms down the Lake to the mill. When going through locks at the dams, the bundles have to be strung out.

The logs are stored at the lower end of the Lake. Small tugs sort the logs in a similar manner as in coastal operations. Logs destined for the Pope and Talbot Mill below the dam, have to go down through a locking system.

The logs have to be taken down through the locks in the dam in order to get them to the mill. A lot of them are sorted above the dam.

DAVIS RAFT

A problem developed when loggers wanted to get logs to the mills from areas exposed to the open ocean. The flat boom or the standard type of bundle boom, could not be used at sea. Stronger tows were needed. There had been some success on the east coast of the continent in the 1890s with large, cigar-shaped rafts. The logs were wired and chained together. This method was brought to the west coast.

In 1893, a giant "Joggins Raft" was built in Coos Bay on the Oregon coast. It contained 5 million board feet. The tug, Ranger, took off with it in November for California. One can only imagine what a dreadful experience it would be to take off with such a gigantic tow in the winter time. That stretch of water is not exactly easy going at the best of times. The unwieldy tow wound up aground inside the bar. The Ranger damaged its rudder in the process. On the next try the engine broke down. After the engine was repaired, the raft grounded on the bar. When the tug got it off, the crew had to let the towline go before the monster towed the tug backward over the sand bars. A storm came up to add to their troubles.

A big vessel, named the National City, took over the tow and got it on its way. This was not a fast moving tow. A storm came up off Cape Mendocino and completely destroyed the weakened raft.

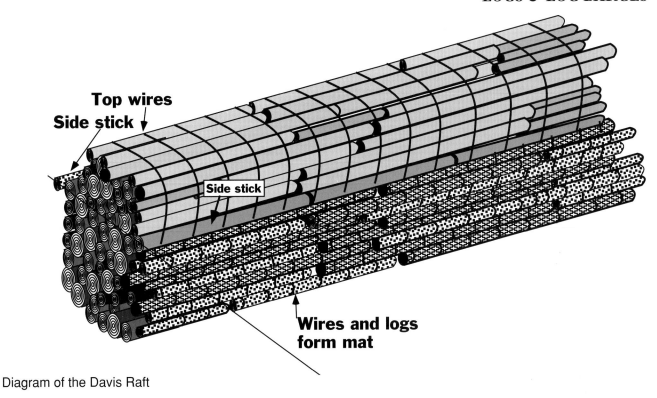

Top wires
Side stick ↓
Side stick
**Wires and logs
form mat**

Diagram of the Davis Raft

The next raft was built on the Columbia River above Astoria. This one was 525 feet long (160 m.) and had a draft of 20 feet. It also was made up of 5 million feet of Douglas fir. A ship's anchor chain ran the length of the raft. Other chains were wrapped around the raft every twelve feet. The tug, Monarch, took off with the raft and a series of storms destroyed it before it got too far. Despite the terrible odds of a tow like that succeeding, the crew was blamed for the loss.

A third and bigger raft made it to San Francisco in August of 1895. Other tows were made to California but a lot of the timber went on lumber schooners instead. Smaller rafts were successfully used on the Washington coast for years. They were also used to move wood down from Alaska.

In 1906, Benson Evenson devised the Benson Raft. This was a large, cigar-shaped raft. It was built in a cradle and had a towing chain running the length of it. The whole thing was wrapped in chains. These rafts were around 1,000 feet (305 m.) long, 55 feet wide and 35 feet deep. These were very successful rafts but only certain lengths of timber could be transported by them. These rafts towed to San Diego and San Francisco.

In British Columbia, there were several types of these rafts developed. The best known was the Davis Raft, developed in 1911 at Port Renfrew. The method of building these rafts was patented by the inventors, Otis Davis and his brother. The size of these rafts depended on where they were built. A boom stick is 66 feet long (20 m.) so the length of the raft depended on the number of sticks that the booming ground could handle. Port Renfrew could not work more than two sticks long. In the Queen Charlottes, some of them were 5 sticks long containing around 3 million board feet of timber. The earlier Davis Rafts were usually 150 to 250 feet (46 to 76 m.) long.

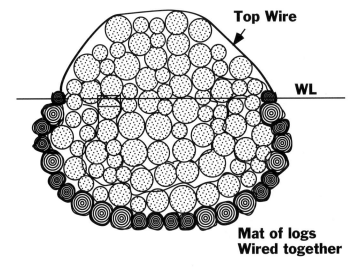

Top Wire

WL

**Mat of logs
Wired together**

Empty self-loading and self-dumping log barge.
The log barge replaced the Davis Raft and most of the long-haul and open-water log towing.

The raft was made by first weaving a mat of logs with wire. Loose logs were piled on top. Then the whole thing was tied together with more wire. There would be up to a million board feet in one of them. Eventually, some of them were 2.5 million board feet and 500 feet (152 m.) long.

Building these huge rafts required a specially skilled crew. A crew of twenty men was needed to build the large rafts in the Queen Charlottes. As with other rafts, there were some variations in construction methods. A mat of logs was made up between two sidesticks and 1.5 inch (3.8 cm.) wire was run over and under each log. By weaving these wires over and under alternate logs, the wires formed a figure of eight. The wires were then made fast to the sidesticks. Layers of logs were placed on top of the mat. This could be done with a crane or other rigging. Each layer was two logs less than the previous layer. The weight of the logs forced the mat down. When enough logs were piled up so you could not put anymore on without sinking the sidesticks, topwires were put on and cinched up to the sidesticks. Some of the wires were known as master or control wires that kept the raft in shape. Other top wires were added afterwards.

British Wire Ropes made up sets of wires for building rafts. They were made up of 11/8 inch (2.9 cm.) or 11/4 (3.2 cm.) diameter wire 137 feet (42 m.) to 160 feet (49 m.) long with a 12 inch (.3 m.) eye on each end. There were 72 wires to a set.

Breaking them up on arrival was not easy. The top wires would be pulled off first. These were coiled up for transportation back to the camp. The master wires were left till last. These held all the weight of the logs. The shackles holding them had their pins blasted out with black powder.

Barge loading operations go on night and day until the barge is loaded. The loaders are flown in and, as soon as the barge is loaded, flown out. The tug immediately heaves the anchors and gets under way.

The logs would spread out while others would surface with great force. One would not want to be standing on the raft when this happened.

The patent was bought by an American company. The rafts were used for years in U.S. waters. Foss was towing small Davis Rafts out of Neah Bay years after they had been discontinued in British Columbia.

The Gibson Raft was also used on the west coast. These rafts used layers of logs tied together by wire. They could work in a small swell without falling apart. They still needed good weather and if a heavy swell or a gale came up, the sticks and wires would break. The first raft was towed across Hecate Strait in 1917 by the Progressive.

Large powerful tugs were needed for these heavy tows. Tugs would wait indefinitely to get a spell of good weather. Getting a tow from the Queen Charlotte Islands and across Hecate Strait, never known for long periods of good weather, took a long time. In good weather the big tugs would move as many booms across Hecate Strait as possible. Then the tows would be moved down the inside. The next wait would be trying to get across Queen Charlotte Sound. When the tug got them inside she had to work the heavy tows down Johnstone Strait and through the Yaculta Rapids. This meant working the back eddies and waiting tide. Kingcome usually towed them to Teakerne Arm where they would be broken up and made into flat booms.

On the west coast of Vancouver Island, the tugs would work their heavy tows from inlet to inlet when they got a break in the weather.

When the self-dumping log barges arrived, the big rafts became a thing of the past. A heavy type of bundle boom replaced them in Port Renfrew where the Davis Raft was born.

LOG BARGES

The first barges used for moving logs were old sailing ships. They had a crew (bargees) on them for steering. Island Tug converted thirteen steel and wood sailing ships into log barges and a large chip barge. They were not the only company to do this. A number of other old ships were tried without too much success. Some of them were lost while under tow. This gave the companies the experience they needed for future barges.

The problem with these vessels, while they took more weather and moved a lot faster than a Davis Raft, was not only the smaller load but they took a long time to load and unload.

Island Tug brought some old tankers from South America. They were converted into self-dumpers greatly reducing the unloading time. Barges were then built by several companies expressly for the trade. The next step was the self-loader.

Log barges are a specialty barge. Most of the ones in service today are self-loaders and self-dumpers. That is, they have cranes on twin towers for loading the logs and tipping tanks for dumping. They are equipped with their own boom boats and have bright lights on the towers for working at night.

They are large, usually over 300 feet (91 m.) long. The largest one, the Seaspan Forester, has a capacity of

The 453 x 96 ft. (138 x 29 m.) Seaspan Forester. She has a capacity of 20,000 tons.

20,000 tons deadweight or four million board feet. The decks are strengthened for the extra punishment they get when loading and dumping. Most of the older non-self-loading barges wound up doing other things such as transporting trailers, containers or general cargo.

When one of the self-loading barges arrives at an up coast camp, it is secured to buoys or sticks. The anchors on the barge and the tug are dropped for security. The tug keeps her towline on the barge during loading. The crew starts to work unlashing boom boats.

The loaders are flown up to the camp. As soon as they are on board, they start clearing the cranes for use. The boom boats are put in the water while the camp makes sure logs are brought alongside the barge. The crew runs the boom boats keeping the logs under the cranes. The logs are picked up with grapples and swung up on the barge. A lot of skill goes into loading a barge. If it is not high enough, it will not dump properly or if it is top heavy, the barge will be unstable and dump out in the ocean.

With the aid of big lights, this loading operation goes on night and day. The cook has hot food for all the men and there is a coffee pot on the stove at all times. The skipper is usually up the whole time the barge is loading.

Barge starting to dump. The earlier barges did not have any cranes for loading. The barges of this type were dumped by a mate or other crew member going aboard and opening a tipping valve.

One of the Crown Zellerbach non-self-loaders in the Jervis Inlet area. The cranes on a self-loader take up room so a lot of the smaller barges were not fitted with them. On the big barges, the crew operates boom boats in order to keep a supply of logs under the cranes. On this type of barge, the tug is often towing something else while the barge is loading.

As soon as the barge is loaded and the boom boats are stowed, the loaders go ashore to get a flight back. The anchors are raised and the barge is let go. The tug is on her way down the coast to the dumping ground. As soon as the on-watch mate and the seaman have washed up, they will be in the wheelhouse to take over the watch.

The barge may take some time to get to the dumping ground. The big ones will take a lot of weather but the smaller barges may have to take it easy if a gale is blowing and there is a heavy swell running. Some of them dumped at sea when they pushed the weather too much. A poorly loaded barge will also cause it to dump prematurely.

The tug brings the barge into the dumping ground at the end of the trip. A small tug puts a line on the stern to hold the barge in place. The large tug keeps a bit of towline out and jogs ahead on the barge. Meanwhile, boom boats get a string of sticks ready to surround the load after it gets in the water. When the barge starts to dump, the small tug quickly lets go of the line. If it can not for some reason, it would be dragged violently backwards and probably sunk. The main tug lets the towline run as the dumping barge takes off. On some of the older and smaller barges, they almost left the water as the heavy load was released.

On the earlier self-dumpers, the mate or another crew member went on the barge to open the dumping valves. These were usually located in the forward part of the barge. When the necessary valves were opened, the mate would go back up on deck while the barge dumped. It took some time for the barge to dump so he could sit and relax for a while. As the barge started to list, the mate got into a good position to hang on tight. When the barge dumped it took off sideways. When things settled down the mate would go down and close off the valves. The diesel pump would be started so the tipping tanks could be pumped dry. On the big, new barges the valves and engines are radio controlled so the crew does not have to go on board; that is if everything works.

Been bothering the loaders again Jones?

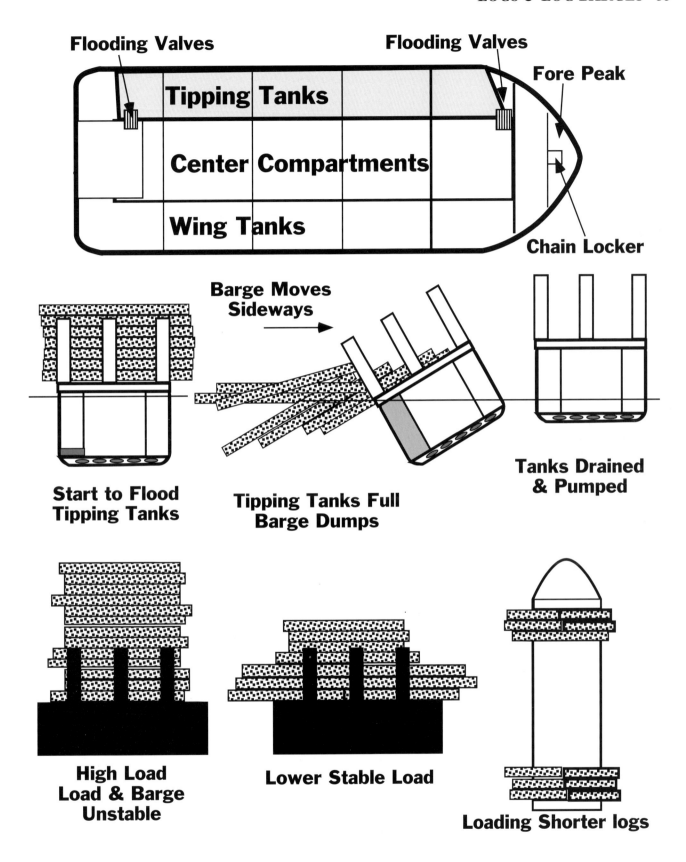

Flooding Valves

Flooding Valves

Fore Peak

Tipping Tanks

Center Compartments

Wing Tanks

Chain Locker

Barge Moves Sideways

Start to Flood Tipping Tanks

Tipping Tanks Full Barge Dumps

Tanks Drained & Pumped

High Load Load & Barge Unstable

Lower Stable Load

Loading Shorter logs

The logs did not always go straight off the barge. Sometimes one of them would wind up on the fore peak. The author got off the barge so he could take a picture of the dump. When he got back on board, he found a large log where he normally would have been standing.

If the dump is not clean, the tug will have to stop and get the rest of the logs off. If a lot of logs are left on, the loaders may have to be called back to remove them using the cranes. If only a few are left, a small tug can be used to pull them off one at a time. The tug crew will go on the barge and hook up rigging for the small boat. Explosives were tried at one time to try and blow the logs off. This was discontinued when, surprising as it might seem, deck damage occurred.

The main tug will then shorten up and start the pumping process. If it is a clean dump, she will slowly start on her way back to the next job. When the barge is righted and the engine shut down, the tug will run line and head at full speed back up the coast for another load.

These barges are big. Towing them needs special care. This is another specialized part of the industry. The men engaged in this type of towing may not be at home with a big bundle tow behind them just as most logtowers would not feel at home with a huge barge.

Top: Barge starting to dump her load.
Bottom: The load is gone. The barge goes sideways through the water.
Right: Sometimes the barge won't dump or part of the load is left on.

Rivtow Carrier dumping in Howe Sound. On arrival of the tug and the barge they proceed to the designated dumping area. A small tug puts a line on the stern of the barge to stop it. The tug and the small tug pull against each other to keep the barge in position until it dumps. The dumping valves are opened and the barge starts to list. When it is far enough over, the load will dump. The small boat must drop her line and the tug must run line. Boom boats are ready with a string of sticks to surround the logs.

5
SCOWS & BARGES

The Nitinat Chief getting ready to pass off a hogger (a scow loaded with hog fuel) to another tug. As a rule, one bridle is dropped as the tug approaches the stern of the receiving tug. The bridles of the receiving tug are put on as the scow comes up to her stern before it takes off. The remaining bridle off the delivery tug is quickly thrown off before everything comes up tight. The receiving tug may already have one or two scows on her towline.

Tugs will often pick up or drop off several scows in a voyage. It saves time if other boats deliver or pick up scows from a tug in route. Smaller tugs are often used to do this in areas where the larger tug can not operate.

Note the coal oil light on the top of the load. Now all lights are battery operated.

The Nitinat Chief is 64 ft. (20 m.) long and at this time had a 400 hp. direct-reversable Washington engine. She was owned by Bill Sorenson before Island Tug purchased her. The tug was built for towing out of Nitinat Lake. While shallow draft for a tug of this size, she drew a bit much for a lot of bar conditions going into the Lake.

Nitinat Lake, on the west coast of Vancouver Island, is a freshwater lake connected to the ocean. A vessel must cross a bar on the way in or out of the Lake. The ocean swell can build up on the bar. Many a vessel has met an untimely end by misjudging the bar conditions.

A couple of examples of wooden scows. The top one is tied up to a boom in Victoria. In order to keep scows in deep water, booms were laid along the dolphins. Heavy lines were also shackled to the booms to secure the scows. When the mill called for the boom the scows had to be shifted, the lines removed and a replacement boom brought in before the scows could be returned. This kept the harbour boats busy for a few hours.

The Wasp, taking an empty chipper to a mill up the North Arm of the Fraser River.

WOODEN SCOWS & BARGES

What is the difference between a scow and a barge. Technically they are all barges but, in British Columbia, a scow usually means a square-ended barge. It seems the term, scow, originated from a flat-bottomed, square-sided sailing vessel.

Wooden scows, of one type or another, were used from the earliest days to move equipment and supplies to isolated locations and bulk products around the coast. Wooden scows served the industry well for many years. While they were certainly not trouble free, millions of tons of coal, rock, chips, gravel and many other cargos reached their destinations on them. They formed the floating base for all sorts of equipment such as pile drivers, A-frames, pump scows, fish camps and even floating offices. As with all wooden vessels, there were size restrictions.

The sides of the scow where traditionally flat while the ends were usually raked. Wooden stanchions rose up through the deck to hold the cargo usually in a box. A number of scows had skegs installed on the stern to make them steer better.

Like all things marine, there were several methods of construction used. Many wooden scows were built with solid keelsons. That is, the keelsons were built of solid timbers to deck level in order to take the weight of the cargo. These timbers were secured by long drift bolts. The sides of the scow were built the same way. Heavy, thwartship timbers and bumper timbers held the sides and keelsons together at the bow and stern. They served to absorb the many shocks that the scow would take. Deck beams also held the keelsons and sides together as did other thwartship timbers placed at a lower level. The construction may have included cross-bracing with wood or metal. This form of construction resulted in a number of parallel compartments. Limber holes were cut in the keelsons in order to let bilge water go to the low side for pumping out.

At each end, heavy square timbers that ran from the bottom of the scow to a few feet above deck level were installed. These were the towing posts. On some scows, heavy steel towing bitts were fitted instead. They were so well secured that they could not be pulled out without destroying the vessel. On some scows, stanchions (solid vertical timbers) were placed at deck level while on others, the stanchions went to the bottom. These timbers held the box planks. The height was determined by the type of cargo for which the scow was designed. Rock and gravel scows had short stanchions while a "chipper" had very long ones.

A false deck was built over the actual deck to take the wear and tear of the cargo. Decks were very hard to keep watertight. They took a terrible beating and were dry for long periods then wet again. This meant, if heavy seas started coming on deck, the scow would usually start taking on water.

There were round holes cut into the deck at each corner of the scow for sounding and pumping. When not in use, the hole was filled with a tapered plug, known as a "scow plug." Vent pipes were placed alongside a stanchion in each compartment for ventilation. The bow of the scow often had an extra layer of planking (rake sheathing) installed to reduce the amount of damage caused by the sea

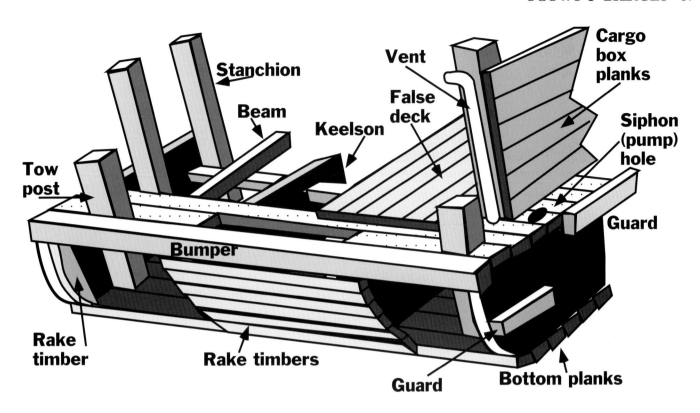

The wooden scow. This was the most common type of construction. Some areas had other names for some of the parts.

and contact with tugs and other barges. Fender planking (whisker guards) were often installed at the corners for the same reason. Heavy horizontal timbers (guards) were secured to the sides of the scow at deck level and at one or more levels along the sides to protect the planking.

A number of scows had a lot of metal reinforcing while others had very little. Nearly all scows had nose irons at each corner. They were a metal strap secured to the deck and bent over the end of the scow.

Some scows did not have the solid keelsons but had support timbers running in different directions. They were a pain in the neck for crews working inside them as they had to crawl under or over these timbers every few feet.

Scows were caulked with oakum and frequently tarred down to the light waterline. Antifouling paint was frequently used below the waterline.

Wooden scows kept towboat crews from getting bored. They were subject to rot, teredos, twisting, not to mention leaking. Loaded, they would not take much weather. They usually did not steer well, to put it mildly.

Water in the hull was a constant problem. If the crew could not get the scow pumped out in time, it would roll over dumping its load. It was quite a sight to watch as the scow started to take on a severe list till it dumped its load. With its weight gone, the scow would nearly jump clear of the water landing upside down. With the remains of the box dragging in the water, capsized scows were very hard to tow. If you were lucky, the bridles stayed on. If not, the crew had to get on the slippery bottom and secure a set of bridles to the bottom with spikes or try to get a wire

When repairs had to be done inside the scow, a hatch consisting of a caulked plank was lifted. The crew members lowered themselves inside the scow.

Right: Showing construction details on wooden scows. The top left type with solid keelsons was the most common.

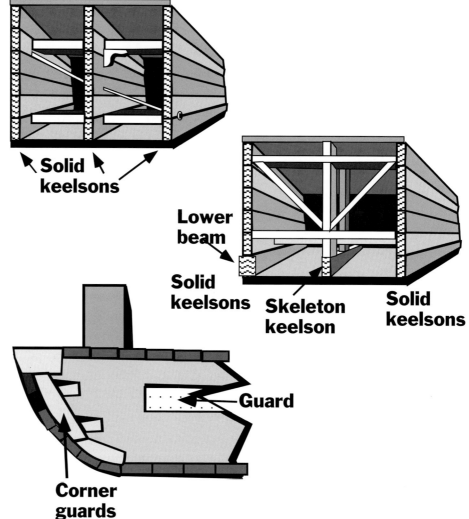

Solid keelsons

Lower beam

Solid keelsons   **Skeleton keelson**   **Solid keelsons**

Guard

Corner guards

around the underwater tow posts. As a rule, the tug had another scow to look after as well. When coupling gear was used, the couplers could fall off the overturned scow leaving the other adrift. If you were not too lucky, this second barge could take a run at the sunken scow. If they connected, it would mean damage to the second scow. The crew then had two decrepit barges. If the vents on a leaking scow were plugged for some reason, the air pressure inside would increase till it exploded. This could throw planks for some distance.

If loaded scows started leaking tied up to the dock, they could still do a lot of damage. One coal barge tied up in Victoria started to leak. As it went down, the tieup lines broke. The wind blew it down to the next dock where it took out the loading ramp. It continued on to a small boat yard where it sank three boats then rolled over dumping its load in the harbour. Several people were not overly impressed with this.

Towboat crews became adept at pumping and patching scows. On steam tugs, steam syphons were used

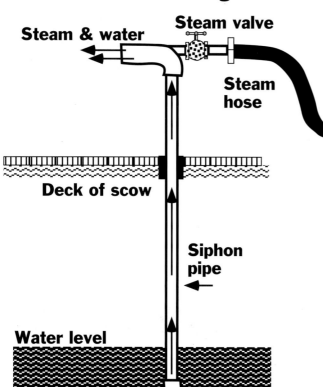

Steam & water   **Steam valve**

Steam hose

Deck of scow

Siphon pipe

Water level

Left: A steam siphon. For years this was used on the steamers to pump out scows. Steam from the hose escaped out the pipe dragging air with it. This reduced pressure in the long pipe. The reduced pressure in the pipe dragged the water up and over the side.

to dewater the scows. This consisted of a long, metal tube that would reach from the sounding hole to the bottom of the barge. A steam fitting was installed at the top. Steam hoses were run from the tug to the syphon. When steam pressure was applied, it reduced the air pressure in the tube creating a syphoning effect. These syphons were very efficient. A tug could run several of these at a time.

The low side of the scow was pumped first. If the deck was slightly underwater when they started, one man stood by with a rigged syphon while the other man knocked out the scow plug. As soon as the hole was cleared, the syphon was jammed down the hole and the steam turned on. Sacks and rags were jammed in around the syphon to reduce the amount of water down flooding the scow. If the leak was not too bad, the deck would come above water level. If the deck was not rising, other syphons would have to be put into service. If the barge was still taking on water faster than it could be pumped out, the crew had to be ready to get off before it rolled. If possible, the tug was brought alongside for pumping but if in open water or the barge was too far over, the crew had to pack all the equipment back to the scow.

Later on, gas pumps were used as well. There have been vast improvements in gas pumps over the years but at first, they were very temperamental. Regardless of the number of times you ran the pump on deck to make sure it was working well, you could bet it would not start out on the scow. When diesel boats came along, gas pumps were the main way of pumping scows, though a lot of tugs today have syphons that work off their main fire pumps.

Often loads had to be pumped out every day even under normal conditions. Needless to say, the crews were efficient at pump drill. One observer remarked that scow-boat men looked like the fire department. Wooden scows had to be watched constantly. The tug would never depart with loads until the crew had sounded and, if necessary, pumped each barge. If there was much water, the crew would listen for the sound of running water in the vent pipes. This would indicate a leaking scow.

Of course pumping alone was often not enough. The crew would have to go down inside the scow and patch it. Hatches were lifted at the end of the scow to gain entry to the hull. The crew wandered around in the dark bowels of the barge looking for signs of running water. Sometimes leaks were easy to find, but often required a little detective work. If your flashlight went out while you were at the far end of the scow, it was a long, wet trip groping your way back to daylight.

Working on the inside of the barges was often a wet, miserable job. On one old sinking scow in Nanaimo Harbour, a green deck hand was surprised to find he was alone down there patching a hole while the experienced hands stayed on deck giving orders. Much later, he found out that the deck of the barge was so rotten that the skipper and mate thought it might collapse. They sent the new guy down because he did not know any better and was considered expendable if things went wrong.

On the Columbia River, the skipper and mate were patching the inside of a wooden scow when the load shifted. The scow rolled over killing the trapped men. While this was a rare case, we have all had to beat a hasty retreat when the water started to rise.

Pumping wooden scows on a steam tug.
The plug was knocked out and the scow sounded with a long pole. The siphon was lowered in the hole. The steam hose was connected. After steam was in the hose, the valve on the siphon was opened. When water started to shoot out, the steam pressure was reduced.

Above: River tug taking two scows through a swing bridge in the North Arm of the Fraser River.
Below: Lumber scow alongside a ship in Victoria.

Watch the bump fellas!

Steel flat scow (low box) loaded with rock. These barges have a lot of rake which makes them tow well on a long line. They yaw a lot on a short line and the rake can do a lot of damage when they are yarded.

Large chip barge loading near Aberdeen, Washington. She has a heavy box which she will need if she is towed over the bar at the entrance to Grays Harbor into the open Pacific.

Scow tieup in the Fraser River. River boats bring loaded scows from the mills and take empties back up. The outside tugs pick up the loads after tying up the empties.

STEEL SCOWS

As the need for larger cargos increased, more and more scows were built of steel. This reduced many problems associated with wood. They could operate in heavier seas and were not subject to rot and worms.

There are a variety of construction methods employed in steel scow construction. Most of them have a frame work of heavy steel frames, floors and beams strengthened by heavy fore and aft stringers. Steel plate is welded to this framework. Heavier strengthening plates are located at points of stress, such as where the tow bitts are located. The scow is divided into several tanks. There is usually a fore and aft bulkhead running the length of the barge. Thwartship bulkheads are installed at intervals the length of the barge. These bulkheads form the sides of the tanks. Each tank will have a manhole and pump hole for repairing and pumping purposes.

Steel scows are not completely trouble free however. Steel rusts and can get holes punched in it from contact with other barges, the bottom or docks. Mind you, if a particular barge suddenly gets too many of these holes from the above effects, the skipper may find himself sailing as mate. The crews still have to know how to pump out scows and go down inside to patch them. A lot of scow boats pack salvage material for this purpose. Slopping around looking for leaks in the bottom of a steel scow has not improved over the wooden ones. In fact, the air is often worse and possibly dangerous.

The earlier steel scows had wooden fenders placed at various heights along the sides of the barges. This practice has been discontinued on most newer barges. Stanchions are normally welded to the deck. The tow bitts, fore and aft, are held in place with heavy welds. There may be fairleads lined up with the tow bitts to reduce wear on the towing bridles.

Nearly all modern scows have skegs which look and act like large, immovable rudders. In the days of the wooden scow and earlier steel scows, they were straight fore and aft. On modern scows, they are shaped to make the barge tow straighter if it is loaded properly. The least yawing a scow does the less power is needed to get it up to a given speed.

The shape of the barge's bow as with any vessel, makes a big difference in its speed through the water. The best shape is the one with large rakes. Unfortunately, these bows do a lot of damage to other barges when yarding or juggling and have been known to crush the housework on the odd tug. They often yaw a lot when towed on a short line. Most of the modern barges do not have this large a rake.

The "chipper" is an example of an ordinary scow with a high box on it. The same design of scow but with a low box is used for gravel and rock. This barge can also be used for lumber and other bulk cargos.

The scows get bigger all the time. With steamboats and wooden scows a tug might tow one scow with 500 tons of cargo and another with 250 tons. These days a lot of the scows will have at least 4,000 tons of cargo. A 1,200 hp. tug will normally tow three chippers each having 2,100 tons or more of cargo.

New steel barges have been built in China and towed across the Pacific. They are 212 ft. (65 m.) x 52 x 13 feet with a 3,000 ton capacity.

STEEL BARGES

As we mentioned before, scows and barges are often referred to as barges. Technically, a scow is "a beamy flat-bottomed vessel used in sheltered waters for freighting or lighterage purposes;" while a barge is a heavy freight boat with no motive power. The distinction blurs in modern usage. Usually, barges are larger than scows.

At first, most barges were converted ships. Unfortunately, ships are not designed to be towed and can give the towboat a lot of problems. Old passenger boats were some of the worst to steer. Some towed better backwards. The ex-passenger ships had very fine bows (small entrance angle) and a small beam for their length. A lot of the old sailing ships converted to barges had a crew on them. The barges were steered so they would not sheer too much. The tankers were notable exceptions to this. Island Tug converted them to self-dumping log barges. Proper skegs were installed to make them steer well.

Very large and speciality barges will have different shapes and construction methods. They often look like ships' hulls and are as big or bigger than WW11 freighters. Large barges will have their own anchoring systems including engines for running anchor winches, pumps and lights. Some of these activities can be operated by the tug with radio control. Some of them have their own equipment for loading or unloading. Some of them are semi-submersibles. That is, tanks can be flooded for loading and then pumped out for sea.

Some types of barges built for special use are log barges and rail or "car barges" that can be seen all over the coast. Paper barges, ranging in size from 200 feet (61 m.) to large ocean-going barges, and oil and chemical barges are all built for one purpose. The construction methods vary but many of them are constructed in the same manner as a ship of similar tonnage.

THE CARGOS

There are a lot of cargos handled on scows and barges. Lumber, machinery and coal were some of the first. It would be impossible to list all the cargos that have been shipped by barge, but we shall mention a few of them.

COAL

For years, towing coal scows was an important part of the towboat industry. Coal is still shipped by barge from Quinsam Coal near Campbell River. The modern conveyor on the dock can load a large barge in a few hours. At one time, small wooden scows moved most of the coal around the coast.

The discovery of commercial quantities of coal in 1852 on Vancouver Island, and the start of the mines had a large effect on the economy and on the shipping industry. The H.B.C. started the mining operations in what is now Nanaimo but sold them in 1862 to the Vancouver Coal

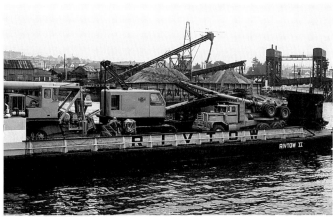

A scow load of sixties-type machinery headed for a logging camp. Machinery is transported all over the coast on scows.

Foss tug with barge in Port Townsend. The pulp mills take advantage of the tug and barge concept in a number of ways. Product is often transported on barges and fuel and supplies are delivered to the mills.

Above: Tug towing oil scow. These scows supplied fuel to vessels in bays and inlets along the coast.
Below: Tug yarding a load, Powell River.

An empty rock barge towed by the wooden tug, Island Monarch. These barges are loaded with rock at Texada Island and towed to the Columbia River for unloading near Portland.

The Union Bay dock.
The deep-water ship and the tug were probably both loading coal. Note the rail cars on the top of the dock.
Courtenay Museum

Loading coal at Union Bay on the outside of the dock. The conveyor was used by this time. Originally, the coal came down chutes one car load at a time. The tug crew moved the scows up and down the dock with hand winches.
Courtenay Museum

Mining and Land Company. The company brought miners and their families out from Britain. A second company known as the Dunsmuir, Dingle and Company started in 1869. The Dunsmuirs made a fortune on coal and the mistreatment of the miners.

A railway was built to move supplies up and down the island. Wharves were built in Departure Bay. Due to problems with railway rights-of-way involving the two companies, in 1899 Dunsmuir was forced to build loading facilities at Ladysmith.

In 1888, the Union Mines were opened in Cumberland. In the same year, construction started on the loading wharf and trestle in Union Bay.

For many years coal was shipped from Ladysmith, Nanaimo, and Union Bay in ships, barges and on scows. Union Bay was the last of these old coal ports in operation. Dunsmuir had a large tug, named the Lorne, to tow sailing ships to the coal ports. There were many other tugs engaged in the very competitive business of towing the sailing ships. In most cases, they were towed from Juan de Fuca Strait and back again after they were loaded. Some ships were converted to barges for moving coal around the coast. The Robert Kerr, was one of these ships. In 1911, she hit part of what is now known as Miami Reef while under tow of the tug, Coulti in route from Ladysmith to Vancouver. She was originally a British bark that was converted to a barge after stranding near San Juan Island in 1885.

Marpole Towing, Victoria Tug and later Island Tug were some of the companies engaged in towing coal scows on the coast for years. Victoria Tug towed to Victoria, Bamberton and Seattle while Marpole Towing mainly serviced the Vancouver area.

LOADING COAL AT UNION BAY

The Union Bay dock was built of wooden timbers in two levels. Rail cars from the mine were run out on the top level for dumping. The lower level was similar to most docks used by ships. On the upper level a winch was used to move the cars over the holes in the decking for the conveyor or chutes on each track. The dock was used for loading deep-sea ships, scows and bunkering coal burners. Originally, it extended 560 feet (171 m.) out into the bay. In 1910, the wharf was extended. It was 48 feet wide (15 m.) with 3 rail tracks. It could stand the weight of a 100 ton locomotive and cars.

The coal cars were built with doors in the bottom that could be opened with a bit of perseverance from the side. The coal often had to be dislodged with bars and hammers. Chinese dumpers worked hard at getting the coal out of the cars especially when dumping fine coal for the cement plant at Bamberton. In cold weather, the cars would freeze taking longer than ever to dump.

The metal chutes were used for years before the conveyor was built. They were lowered down at an angle to let the coal run down to the ship or scow below. By altering the angle of the chute, the coal would, in theory, land near the center of the scow. If the car dumped quickly, the coal could land on one side of the scow before the crew had a chance to move it. A series of buckets could be attached to one of these chutes for bunkering up tugs and coasters.

Seaspan Cavalier, getting away with a tow at Seaspan, North Vancouver.

The conveyor was much more reliable. It could be moved in or out to give much more control over where the coal landed though the crews had to still move the scow with lines. The conveyor was used for loading scows if there were no ships alongside the dock.

The tug would usually arrive in the bay with two empty wooden scows early in the morning. The crew would shorten up the heavy, wet, manila couplers used to tow the second scow and get the long loading lines ready. When the scows were alongside the dock, the loading lines were run up on the lower dock. The tug "spotted" the first scow under the conveyor or chute. Wire winch lines were run out to opposite ends of the scow.

As the coal was loaded, the scow had to be shifted up and down the dock by the crew using the hand winches. In order to keep the scow level, it generally had to be pushed off the dock with a pole and block and tackle. When a strong southeaster was blowing, extra lines were run out to keep the barges from breaking adrift. When the scow was loaded, it was measured for freeboard. If it was not level, the deck hands and the mate got to work with shovels on the coal piles and corrected it.

The towboat crews were normally good at climbing around these scows and handling all the lines but some had a bit of a problem adapting. A green deckhand had a bad day. He started by copying the cigar-smoking mate and lit up a stogy. As a nonsmoker, this was not a good idea. When it was time for lunch the somewhat queasy seaman was reluctant to climb down a ladder or slide down a line like the rest of the crew. The skipper bellowed at him to jump in the coal pile on the scow. They had been loading powdered coal so it would be soft. As the skipper was getting a bit more agitated, the seaman made a panicky jump, unfortunately head first. The crew had to pull him out of the coal pile.

When loading fine coal for the cement plant, straw was placed in the bottom of each rail car in an attempt to

Island Rustler, heading out of Victoria Harbour. Note the Babco Paint factory before it was torn down for a hotel.

The Crofton pulp mill. The mills use all types of shipping for transporting product and receiving supplies. The scows in the background are hung on buoys. The loads used to be tied up to standing sticks which did not allow much space for yarding.
Below: Loading a hog scow on the river.

The Seaspan Queen, with two loads going down the Fraser River. She probably will pick up another scow elsewhere to complete her tow.

It's not bad out here Jim. Things moving around a bit though.

Seaspan Charger, yarding a tow. She needs her 900 hp. when yarding and towing heavy chippers in the river.

keep the coal from running out through the cracks between the doors. This straw wound up on the scow. For years, a Chinese gentleman we called "Two Cup" walked up and down the coal piles removing the straw so it would not create difficulties with the burners in Bamberton.

Loading coal this way was not a fast process. If work started first thing in the morning, the tug would get away with two loaded scows by the middle of the afternoon. One scow would usually have 500 tons and the other 250 tons on board.

When the deep-sea ships were loading or when bunkering up some of the ships, coal trimmers from shore were used in the holds to make sure every corner was filled. Government ships such as, the Estevan and the William J. Stewart, took on bunkers all the time but they used their own crews for trimming like the rest of us. Some of the larger tugs used trimmers as well.

The visiting ships' crews often painted the ship's name and home port on boards which were nailed on the wharf timbers. The crews were from all over the world.

Oil reduced the need for coal and the operation ended in the fifties. The old dock is gone now along with the Chinese men that laboured on it. The sound of rail cars being shunted down the dock and the shouts and laughter of the towboat crews as they worked their scows along the dock, can no longer be heard. The smell of smoke from the stacks of the steamers is gone as well. All is now quiet in the bay.

WOOD CHIPS

As pulp mills became more common on the coast, the need for fibre increased. The lumber mill had a lot of waste material. They could chip the wood for pulp and paper. The bark and other low-grade material could be used for fuel in the pulp mills. All this material had to be transported. Tugs and barges were the most economical on the coast. Special barges were built for this trade. They had very high boxes to contain the light cargo.

At first, a tug would tow two loaded chippers at a time. When high speed diesels were developed, more powerful tugs could tow three of them. On open water, such as the west coast of Vancouver Island, a tug is reduced to two at a time. Mills all over the coast, from Aberdeen on the Washington Coast to Alaska, produce chips and hog fuel which are loaded on these scows.

A tug can make up a tow from several mills before proceeding on to the pulp mill. At times, a tug will take a barge from another tow or meet a harbour tug with a barge to complete her tow.

When they were made of wood, a leaking barge could list and the cargo could shift taking out one side of the box. There were chips and bits of wood all over the place. Meanwhile, the tug had to contend with a crippled or sunken barge. The steel barges reduced the problem but did not eliminate it. Too much sea can damage a box or wash away cargo. If the tug can get into a sheltered bay before the barge goes over far enough to dump everything, the crew can get up on the load and start shoveling chips. They move the load by hand until the barge or barges are level again. Barges that operate in open water have reinforced boxes to reduce damage but most of them will not take much swell.

ROCK AND GRAVEL

Tons of rock and gravel have been shipped by barge. This is one cargo that can be found on the move almost anywhere. Rock and gravel can be found on small gravel scows or large barges with over 10,000 tons of cargo. The large, lime rock barges are towed from Texada Island to the Columbia River. Smaller barges leave Texada for Puget Sound and gulf ports. Gravel scows are often loaded at pits located around the coast and towed to construction sites in Puget Sound and British Columbia.

OIL CHEMICAL

Oil and chemical barges are other forms of specialty barges. They are constructed in the pattern of small tankers. They have their own pumping equipment for loading and discharging cargo. The piping system on an oil barge is quite complex.

Some chemical barges will transport rail as well. Very strict regulations as to the handling of these hazardous products are enforced. There is a difference in some of the construction standards between U.S. and Canada but both countries have high standards. Only qualified people are allowed to load or discharge product. In the U.S. there must be a man with a tankerman's license in charge of these operations. In Canada, the bargeman must meet similar standards.

One of the greatest dreads a skipper has is a towline breaking. As with other barges, a pickup line is attached to a spare towline but this can be hard to pickup in heavy seas. There have been surprisingly few accidents with them. A tug with a damaged barge off the Washington Coast polluted Long Beach on Vancouver Island as well as a few other places.

Loading barges in the Fraser River. The large one is probably going to Prince Rupert.

Rivtow ramp barge arriving Prince Rupert. A variety of cargo is transported from Vancouver by barge.

Harbour tug assisting in Prince Rupert.
Below: Covered barge, Prince Rupert.

Tacoma: A Crowley "Red Stack" tug unloading oil barge. The tug stays alongside the barge as a safety measure while it is off-loading petroleum products.

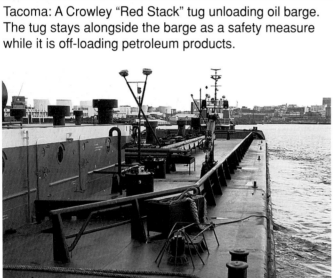

The product is tested before and after it is discharged. Before they were quite as careful, a load of gas was pumped off into a tank that was supposed to contain coal-oil. Fortunately, the error was discovered before anyone set himself on fire while trying to light a lamp.

Chemical barges handle the cargo according to the type of the chemical involved. The tanks can be on deck, in the hull or, in some cases, both. As with all hazardous cargo, chemical barges can not be moved without emergency response forms that let the crew know what to do in an emergency.

Top: The Seaspan Valiant, pumping off at a west coast port. For years her sister ship the Victor, had a steady run to small camps and ports on the west coast.
Above: Oil barge departing Sooke. This operation has gone too, along with the local lumber industry.

An oil barge arriving Victoria.
For years barges brought petroleum products to Victoria. As the tank farms were removed, the number of tugs and barges used decreased accordingly.

Pumping off chemicals at a pulp mill. The chemical, in this case caustic, is pumped before the rail cars can be unloaded. The rail cars usually have other types of chemicals used in the manufacture of pulp and paper. The tugs are very careful when handling this type of cargo. Emergency response forms must accompany all hazardous cargos.

Seaspan 270, 400 ft. (122 m.) long and 100 ft. (30 m.) wide capacity 15,000 metric tons. The 5,750 hp. tug, Seaspan Regent, averaged 10.75 knots from Cowichan Bay, on Vancouver Is. to San Pedro, California with 7,000,000 feet of lumber. This barge had a type of skegs that increased her speed.

Empty paper barge off Pulteney Point, Malcolm Island, heading for Port Alice. She will be loaded for a return trip to Vancouver.

PAPER

Pulp and paper is shipped from the mills to ports such as Vancouver or Seattle. Covered barges are used for this so the product will not get wet. On open-water routes, the paper is stopped from moving in a sea by large inflated bladders. These barges are loaded and unloaded by shore crews though some tug companies get their crews to handle the cargo.

Large ocean-going paper barges. The barge at the top used to be on a steady run from Port Alberni to California. Bottom: Nahmint Carrier.

Puget Sound Freight Services paper barge. They hauled cargo from Puget Sound and B.C. mills. They had barges ranging from 156 to 253 ft. (48 to 77 m.) taking as much as 4,100 tons of cargo.

Paper barges such as this Norsk barge regularly operate between the pulp mills and Vancouver.

Paper barge unloading in Victoria. Pulp and paper is collected in warehouses until there is enough for a ship.

Seaspan 251, loaded with lime rock from Texada Island for the Portland area. Built in 1977, this barge was as big as they could get into the Willamette River where the cement plant was at that time. Length 360 ft. (110 m.) breadth 90 ft. (27 m.) with a draught of 20 ft. (6 m.). The pusher tugs took her from Astoria to the plant.

Load of gravel approaching the locks below Lake Union. Tug, Sovereign, Fremont Tugboat Company.

Evco Spray, headed for the gravel pits near Victoria. This was a steady run for a number of boats but the gravel is running out at this location.

The Julius Brisco, pushing a gravel scow in Seattle.

Gravel from the same pits entering Victoria. The harbour tugs have a steady job loading scows for the city
Right: Loading lime rock at Vananda on Texada Island.

Tug and barge in Grenville Channel heading for Alaska. Supplies of all sorts go north on barges. Many communities in Alaska depend on the barges for most of their supplies. There is far more of this traffic in the summer before the Ice closes more northern harbours.

Cement barge leaving Lafarge Cement Plant in the Fraser River. Bulk cement is transported to many locations in special barges. The cement is discharged through hoses to storage areas ashore.

I wonder if they're trying to tell us something.

RAIL

One type of barge that is seen all over the coast is the rail barge. They were originally wooden barges often towed by large tugs. Since the late fifties, they have been constructed of steel.

In 1855, when rail arrived to Vancouver, it increased the amount of shipping on the B.C. coast and in Puget Sound. This was the reverse of the effect rail had on coastal/river traffic in the eastern part of the continent. It was expensive to lay track in a lot of the rugged terrain in the west.

When coal was discovered in the 1850s, rail was used to get it to loading facilities. The ENN line began in

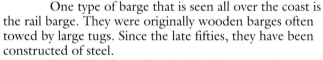

Left: Gulf of Georgia, towing the empty chemical barge, Metlakata, south. This barge supplied the pulp mill in Prince Rupert. She carried 900 tons of chlorine on deck and 3,000 tons of liquid caustic in the hull. Several companies towed her over the years. Rivtow got the contract in 1992.

Island Warrior, 90 ft. (27 m.) 1,530 hp., arriving Seattle. The Warrior and other tugs had a scheduled run for B.C. Railway running rail cars from Squamish and later, North Vancouver to Seattle. The skipper is on top of the rail cars giving steering orders and engine moves to the mate in the wheelhouse.

1883 on Vancouver Island. The loggers soon started using rail to bring the timber to the water.

At first, all cargo was loaded and off loaded to steam ships and barges from the rail cars in Vancouver or on Vancouver Island. The need for moving rail cars to the Island and other out ports increased. The Canadian Pacific Railway had its own tug and barge system for years, as did the Canadian National Railway in later years. The CPR purchased the ENN in 1905 along with the Czar and the Escort No 2. They soon started running rail barges.

When pulp mills were built, it was found that one of the best ways to move chemicals and supplies was by rail cars. In 1912, the Pacific Great Eastern, now B.C. Rail running from Squamish to the interior, was started. Barges moved rail cars from Squamish to Vancouver and other ports until the line was completed to North Vancouver.

Rail barges were used to connect ports in Puget Sound. For many years, rail cars were moved from Seattle to Victoria and Vancouver. Rail cars also go north to connect with rail lines in Alaska.

Most of the barges were built of wood. The wooden barges were quite long for a wooden vessel and suffered from hogging and twisting. To reduce this, a lot of them had a frame of hog chains and timbers on each side of the barge.

At first, a lot of the early car barges had their own crews aboard. They loaded the barge, tied down the rail cars so they would not jump off the rails in bad weather and steered the barge when it was underway. There were living quarters constructed on the stern of the barge with a wheelhouse on top. There were smaller scows fitted with rails for short runs as well. The tugs were usually big and could easily handle a barge alongside. Later, smaller tugs were used and the towboat crew did all the work with the cars.

Right: The rails on the older car barges.

The skipper's view from the top of the cars while making a landing.

Foss tug southbound from Alaska with two car barges.

"Red Stack" tug heading north for Alaska. The rail traffic is a steady business for companies towing very large rail barges. The Hydro Train barges vary in size but most of them are 400 ft. (122 m.) long by 75 ft. (23 m.) wide.

A Foss tug landing a barge in Seattle.

The Seaspan Defender, used as a push tug on the Vancouver to Nanaimo run.

The old wooden barges were heavy to tow and hard to handle. In the late fifties, the wooden barges were replaced by steel barges. The steel barges are usually much bigger and tow easily. While some of them also take chemicals in the hull, most are floating railways. IT 106 was an example of this. Built in 1964, her registered length was 264 ft. (80 m.) with a 15-car capacity. Other barges were converted to car (rail) barges, such as the Island Hemlock with a registered length of 305 ft. (93m.) and a 22-car capacity. Much larger barges were built by the American companies for the Alaskan run. The U.S. tugs on these runs were big and powerful. They could move a couple of barges along faster than anyone would have dreamed of a few years back.

Some Canadian companies built train ships. These were vessels designed to transport rail and trailers only. They replaced a lot of tug and barge-rail operations.

While they have the same basic construction as other barges, the bows often have more rake. The number of cars that can be carried varies a lot from barge to barge, as does the number of tracks on deck.

In most cases, the tug takes the barge alongside for landings. The barge goes into a slip where it can be connected to an apron or ramp. The ramp is lowered on the barge so its rails line up with the rails on the barge. For years, this procedure of lining up the rails was accomplished by manoeuvring the tug and barge. Later, winches were used to speed up the process. As a rule, wire winch lines and heavy turnbuckles hold the barge in place.

The skipper, Captain George Hovell, throwing a heaving line ashore.
Before radios were used, all steering and engine manoeuvres were conveyed to the wheelhouse with hand signals. If the radio goes dead at the last minute, they still come in handy.

When loading or unloading, the railway engine runs idler (empty) cars down on the barge to connect to the cars on the barge. This keeps the heavy engine off the apron.

Getting cars derailed is a common occurrence in the loading and unloading operation. While not too hazardous, it can be frustrating and can wreck any schedule.

When a barge is loaded, the crew check all the brakes on the cars and put the shoes on the rail. If the barge is going any distance, the cars will have to be tied down to the barge with turnbuckles. For open-water trips, the cars are jacked up and tied down to reduce car movement in a swell. The method of doing this varies from company to company. This work is often done by the crew of the tug.

As hazardous cargo, such as chemicals, can be part of the load, the tug has to be extra careful regarding weather and traffic. In some cases, the hull of the barge can also be loaded with chemicals. At one time, before regulations were as stiff as they are today, old barges were used for this service. With the weight of the rail being loaded on the

The engine ashore starts pulling strings of cars off. To keep the barge more or less level when unloading loaded cars, the first string will usually get pulled so some of the cars stay on until the rest of the loads are pulled.

Shoes are put on the tracks and the rail cars are tied down before departure. The gear used for this depends on the company and where the barge is going. If it is going in open water, the cars will be jacked up and turn-buckles will hold the cars down against the jacks. Chains will be secured to the axles on the cars as well. All the gear is checked before the barge gets into open water to make sure nothing has worked loose.

To save time, shore crews will put all this gear on in some ports. The tug crew will do this in most ports.

Don't worry about that mate. We have our emergency response forms aboard.

barge, caustic chemicals could seep through cracks in the deck. When tying down the cars, the crew could get burned.

One time, someone came up with the idea of getting a crew to clean out the inside of a barge. Safety gear such as rubber pants, jackets and eye protectors were too expensive. While there were major caustic burns, nobody lost their vision.

When the James Island explosives plant was functioning, a tug picked up a barge in Vancouver loaded with chemicals for the Island. The chemicals used in making the dynamite were kept on one side of the Island and the finished product on the other side.

They hooked up the hoses on a chemical car ready for pumping, when they discovered someone had loaded a car full of blasting caps between two nitrate cars. Operations stopped and the tug was told to get the barge around to the other side of the Island as fast as possible.

When the tug and barge started approaching the slip on the powder side, men started waving it off. The tug was told to go back to the other side and get rid of the chemicals. When she got back around, the men on the dock were waving and yelling at the tug to get lost. This procedure went on for hours. There were conference calls back to Ottawa.

The cargo was too dangerous for any port in Canada. The combination of the blasting caps and the nitrates should not have been in the Vancouver area at the same time, let alone on the same old wooden barge. There was enough explosive potential to wipe out the Vancouver waterfront.

The barge was eventually brought into the powder side and the offending car of blasting caps removed. Heads rolled in the C.P.R. over that one.

Car barges are used to supply pulp mills with chemicals and other products. It is not unusual to see a heavily loaded barge heading around to the west coast of Vancouver Island. When the barge arrives at the mill, it may discharge chemicals from its hull before the cars are pulled. The mill engines load the barge with empties for the return trip.

On the Alaskan barges, every type of cargo imaginable can be seen. All cars and cargo are tied down with chain and turnbuckles. Foss and "Red Stack" are some companies engaged in this type of business.

TRAILERS

Trailers are moved back and forth to Vancouver Is. and Powell River on a regular basis. The tractors load and unload the barges at each port. There are several regular runs. Trailers often also make up a large part of the cargo on an Alaskan run.

Lassoing a tow post. This is something every seaman learns to do.

The Lawrence L, arriving Crofton. In ports such as this, if there is no wind, the tug can drop off the head scow and let it drift. The tug then heaves in the pendant and takes the tail scow into the tieup. She will go back and grab the drifting scow in order to tie it up. This works well if the scows go to different tieups. There is too much wind and current in most places for this, so the tug would have to tie up all the scows and yard them later. Now the scows go to buoys, so it would be a lot easier to arrive with several scows.

TOWING SCOWS AND BARGES

The method of towing scows and barges depends on the size of the barge, the size of the tug, its destination and whether the tug is Canadian or American. The American tugs usually use more chain in their towing gear than do the Canadian tugs. Heavy chain bridles that the towline is shackled into are common on all large barges towed in open ocean. These chains are often part of the barge's gear and stay with it. Smaller barges will use chain bridles or combination chain and wire bridles. When towing these barges on inside waters, most Canadian tugs will use wire bridles with soft eyes.

Regardless of the type of loaded barge involved, they are very heavy in relationship to the tug. The tug must approach all landings at a reasonable speed in order to get it stopped or damage will occur.

TOWING WOODEN SCOWS

At one time if the tug had more than one scow, they were hooked together with manila (rope) couplers. These were usually around ten and a half inch circumference, one hundred feet long, with wire pendants on each end. There were shorter versions for harbour and river use. When wet, the couplers were heavy and hard to handle. You never dropped one end in the water because of the weight. On some boats, if a seaman did drop one he had to pull it up by himself. He did not drop it a second time.

Whenever you were going to tie up the scows or if you were going through a narrows, the couplers had to be shortened up. If the skipper was kind, he would back up on the front barge with the tug to get the scows together. If not, the crew would have to pull the barges together with muscle power.

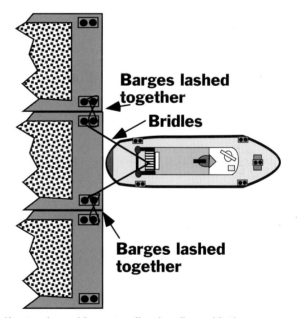

Barges lashed together

Bridles

Barges lashed together

If a tug is making a towline landing with three scows, she can pull them up side by side and lash them together with polypropylene scow lines. The towing bridles are led around the tow bitts of the scows to make a solid unit. The towline is shortened up until the stern of the tug just clears the center scow.

Each tug and skipper will approach the tieup differently. Usually the tug will bring the tow slowly alongside and stop it up by going astern on the scows. The crew will try to get a line from the scow to the tieup. The bridles are thrown off and the tug will push the scows in until the crew makes them all fast. However, things do not always go as simply as this.

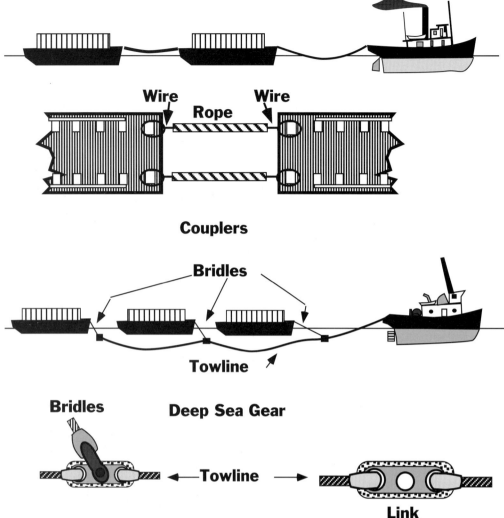

Wire   **Wire**

Rope

Couplers

Bridles

Towline

Deep Sea Gear

Bridles

← **Towline** →

Link

The methods of towing scows and barges in protected and semi-protected waters of the inside passage. At one time, manila couplers were used to connect tandem tows. Eventually deep-sea gear was used except in rivers and harbours. With the use of modern synthetic materials they are used in good weather elsewhere.

The links are placed in the towline so the bridles can be shackled on. If the barges are going on the west coast of Vancouver Island or other areas of open water, the middle link is not used to give more space and towline weight between barges.

Tugs that normally tow large barges in open water will not have links in the line. If they have a tandem tow they will often hook each barge on a separate towline.

At sea the towlines are "tied down" at the stern so they can't jump the pins and get under the counter. This could cause the tug to get into serious trouble.

Ladysmith. Two chippers on couplers. They are handier for short runs and narrow places as the tug has more control over the tow.

The Island Trooper, assisted by the Island Rocket, taking an empty into the mill in Victoria. The Rocket will tail the scow through the bridge and stop it up on arrival. When the mills operated in Victoria the larger tugs could not get into them.

Most of the landings were made with the barges alongside. If the tug had more than one scow, she would put one scow on each side of the boat. The position of the barges and how the lines lead is critical when handling alongside. Even with a top wheelhouse, the skipper often could not see over the loads to make the landing, so he would get on top of the load and signal the mate located in the wheelhouse. The mate would interpret these signals and steer or ring for engine manoeuvres. Today, radios are used for this which help reduce the errors most of the time.

Yarding or juggling scows involved the tug and the crew moving barges around with running lines. A running line was a long, light line that could be handled easily. Skippers liked husky deck hands.

The deck hands got proficient at lassoing towposts with the big, heavy, manila scow lines. Lassoing stanchions, bitts and towposts with wet and sometimes frozen deck lines was, and still is, one of the first skills a seaman learns as there is not likely to be anyone around to catch a line for him.

If he missed when there were any onlookers, it was brought to his attention with a few jeers. When yarding in Lake Union a deck hand missed one and had someone call out: "you Canadian cowboys couldn't catch anything."

Three scows southound off Campbell River. They are on deep-sea gear. The towline bridles go to the tail scow. The bridles from the other scows are shackled on to the links. There are around 400 ft. (122 m.) between the barges. The pendants (line between the barges) move up and down in a swell to take the jerk out of the gear that would break the gear. One of the reasons a tug has a lot of towline out is that the weight of the towline works like a big spring. Obviously, any pleasure boat that runs between the barges or the tug and tow is trying to commit suicide.

The earlier boats were not as manoeuvrable as those of today. In most cases, the skipper had to swing the big wooden wheel from hard over to hard over by hand. If he let go of the wheel when the tug was going astern, the force of the water on the rudder would jam it hard over. If the skipper tried to grab the madly spinning wheel, it would break his arm or break the steering gear. Most boats did not have a wheel at the after controls. If the skipper was handling the boat from the after station, he would have to run up to the wheelhouse to change the rudder position. There were not too many fat skippers!

One skipper handling the boat from the after controls did not notice the second scow had drifted in front of him. He gave a signal for half ahead and the boat hit the scow in front of it with a bang. The jar caused the tops of the masts to swing toward each other then snap back. This broke the aerial strung out between the masts. The wire from the aerial wrapped round the captain so he could not reach the engine room signal. Of course the crew did not laugh, not where he could see them that is.

The old wooden scows were often loaded with the assistance of the crews. After the scows were loaded, they would be sounded for water and pumped out if necessary. After coupling them up, the tug would depart. By comparison, today their loads would be very small; in spite of this, they would only make about three knots.

Coal scows from Union Bay on their way to Victoria or Bamberton would have to watch their weather in the gulf. On the way down, they would go through Porlier Pass or Dodd Narrows. Dodd Narrows has strong currents and is quite narrow. The tug would have to wait for slack water in order to get the loads through it. The couplers were shortened up to half length. The tug would get to the hole ahead of tide time and watch for slack water. If it was blowing a lot of westerly, this could cause the tide to turn a few minutes early or, what was worse, it could

The deck hand getting bridles on an empty.

The scow is slowly being towed by the outside tug. When both bridles are on one corner, the larger tugs' bridles will be thrown off. The smaller tug will pull the barge clear and swing over so one bridle can be shifted to the other corner.

This requires coordination of the crew and the skippers. The deck hands must know what to do or serious problems will occur. As with all the towboat industry, the people involved must work together as a team. Switching scows in bad weather can be dangerous if not done well.

Harbour and river tugs often pick up and deliver barges to the outside tugs. This saves time and, in a lot of cases, there may not be enough water or space for the bigger tug.

The Seaspan Master, shortened up off Point Grey. She is probably waiting for the rest of her tow to come out of the river. If she was going to make a landing with the scow, she would have it up short like this. Most Canadian tugs handle the scows on the towline to save time and the amount of men on deck.

Should we call the office or should we row ashore and forget the whole thing?

Deck hand picking up a line off a buoy. The deck hands and mates have to be agile on the barges. The gear is heavy and things do not stay still too long. The crew working on the barge have to be able to think for themselves.

give the appearance of having turned. This caused a few exciting moments with the tug stuck in the narrows bucking tide and the wind trying to force the scows on to the stern of the tug or beach.

You could run empties northbound with the flood, as long as the towline was let to run free after the tow was clear of the hole. A bit of housework was in for repairs and at least one small tug was rolled over before this lesson was learned.

Today, couplers are made out of synthetic material and are light and quick to use in the river. Here, scows must be close-coupled for going through bridges and other tight holes. You will see them used where yard boats are moving scows short distances, and in good weather you may see empties heading down the gulf on couplers. The deck lines now are all synthetics as well, making them stronger and much easier to handle.

A lot of the earlier towing winches did not have spooling gear, especially on the smaller boats. To spool the towline on the drum, the seaman or mate would put an iron crowbar in a hole in the base of the winch and force the line over with the bar. If the line jumped, it would throw the bar up against the seaman if he was not quick enough to get out of its way.

On one of the smaller one-deckhand boats, the mate was shortening up by himself when the engine sped up. This caused the towline to jump the pins. It hit the bar with enough force to throw the mate backwards. Fortunately, he was able to grab the stern bitts before he went over the side. If he had gone over, the boat would have gone on by itself until it hit something.

DEEP-SEA GEAR

Couplers, of course, were of no value on the open water of the outer coast. When towing more than one barge, a separate piece of towline called a pendant was used. One end of the pendant was made fast to the tail barge, the other end to the towline. The second barge was also hooked on to the towline allowing the pendant to go under this barge. The pendant was the same diameter as the towline and was usually stowed below when not needed. This wire had to be hauled out on deck for use. Getting this gear back in without kinking it was not easy. The capstan was used for this along with running wires, chain stoppers and snatch blocks. This type of gear, known as deep-sea gear, was good for the longer trips on the outer coast but not much use for the shorter trips and smaller crews used in inside towing.

Some of the skippers on the scow boats started clamping boom chains to the towline three or four hundred feet from the end. The bridles to the second scow were shackled on to the chain. In this way, the advantages of the deep-sea gear could be used inside. Assorted clamps were invented for this but many of them had the bad habit of slipping. When they slipped, they would revolve round the towline wrapping the bridles up into a twisted mess. After some experiments with splices in the line, links that could be heaved right on the drum were spliced in. The link is a flat piece of plate with wire sockets on each end and a hole big enough for a shackle pin in the middle. This gear made it possible to handle scows a lot faster and with less men on

The Island Chief, with a barge alongside. The barge was originally a tanker before it was towed to Canada and made into a self-dumping log barge. Later it was converted into a rail barge. The Island Chief is an 80.2 ft. (24 m.) single screw 1,200 hp. tug. She has a steering nozzle.

deck. A modern tug will have two links so she can tow three barges inside and two on outside waters.

A new shore captain sent a deep-sea pendant down to a small, one-deckhand boat that did not even have a capstan. There was no way one man could pull in four hundred feet of 7/8 wire with a scow attached without any power. The wire was stowed below to rust and get in the way. When the scow tieup started to fall apart in Vananda, it was wrapped around all the sticks and forgotten.

For open-water towing, some large tugs have two drums on their towing winches. They then hook one barge to each towline.

When towing in swells, the more weight there is in the towing gear the less chance it will part. In addition to reducing jerking on the towline, chain is less subject to wear than soft wire. Scows that are destined for the open water will have a section of chain made fast to the towing bitts. If there is no chain on the scows, the crew will have to pull chain up from the tug by hand. The bridles are shackled into the chains. Another section of chain is put between the bridles and the link. A lot of the American boats use all chain bridles. The larger barges have chain bridles permanently secured to the barge for the tug to hook on to it. This very heavy gear must be moved with winches.

Every area and each company has its own way of landing scows and barges. For a number of reasons, scows are often handled differently in Washington than in British Columbia. There can be a difference in terminology as well. A lot of the American boats "make up to," or put it "on the hip," ("pick up" Canadian term) a barge or scow. That is, the tug is made fast alongside the barge with a spring line, head line, stern line and possibly a backing line. Many of the Canadian tugs have a smaller tug and crew to work with so they do a lot of towline landings.

If there is more than one scow, they are pulled up side by side and all landed with a towline landing. The bri-

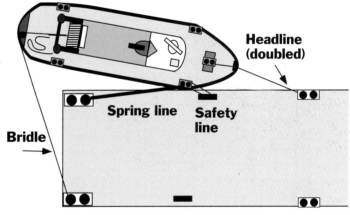

The way a tug picks up (makes up to) a barge will depend on the barge and the tug but these are the main lines used. Some tugs have winches for the headline. Twin screw boats handle barges much better than the single screw tugs. Bow thrusters are being installed on some of the tugs now.

The new tractor tugs will make it easier to handle barges alongside.

Below: LeMars, 95 ft. (29 m.) 1,800 hp.,Vancouver Tug.

"Red Stack" 7,200 hp. tug, Adventure, off Astoria. She came across the Columbia River bar with the barge on her towline. She then made up to her barge. A smaller tug assisted her through the bridge. She is now on her way upriver. Note: She is well back on her tow. A large powerful tug can handle a barge well in this manner.

Tug waiting to go through the locks in the Lake Washington Ship Canal. This tug is designed for push towing.

dles are heaved up on the winch until the stern of the tug just clears the scow. The tug stops the tow by going astern on it. If you angle the stern in a bit while you are going astern, it will push the tow toward the dock so a seaman or mate can get a line on it. At one time, you could not pull the bridles up on the winch which made things a bit dicey.

Whichever method is used, a lot of skill and judgment is required. There is enough weight in the smallest tow to do a lot of damage to a dock. We have noticed the owners of the dock are not amused if you knock out a bunch of expensive piles. Time is also a factor. The towboat companies keep track of how much time a tug takes in delivering a tow and getting away with the next one.

If you are landing a barge with the tug alongside the barge, the skipper or mate will often have to go out on the barge and give manoeuvres to the wheelhouse as visibility usually is restricted. For years, this was done with hand signals but now radios are used. Radios do not mean perfect communication. There seems to be a law that just as you get a few feet off the dock, the radio gets full of static. Once in a while, some guy ashore gets on the same frequency and adds a few extra engine manoeuvres. It is not hard to see why we are not amused when trying to get a barge loaded with chemicals alongside a dock without damage.

Large barges are usually handled alongside on both sides of the border. You can land a 270 ft. (82 m.) barge on the towline with a 75 ft. (23 m.) tug if you have an assist tug to stop it up for you. Several small harbour tugs can handle a barge of this size if there is not too much wind.

The use of push towing is a little more common in the United States than in Canada. In the east, large pusher tugs and barge systems are more common than on the west coast. However, push towing is used on Canadian lakes. Some scows have notches for the bow of the tug. Lines are run from the stern of the tug to the outside corners of the barge. The lines are tightened up with the winch. Large oil barges have successfully operated on the B.C. coast while being pushed, and for a while some rail barges were pushed as well.

In a number of areas like the Fraser River, it is difficult to manoeuvre with three scows strung out. Small river boats will bring the barges down to the larger boat. For a time, boats were attempting to go in and out of the North Arm with three barges strung out and no assist boats. This led to some exciting times and a bit of costly damage. At times it can be entertaining, with two barges on deep-sea gear competing for space with logtowers and other scow boats.

Getting away and heading down the River from New Westminster in freshet time, with an ebb tide, can keep the skipper on his toes. Once he starts the operation he probably will not be able to stop till he gets to the Sand Heads.

Some ports, such as Duncan Bay, can be difficult when arriving with a tow. Due to its proximity to Seymour

The Island Monarch, formally the Seaspan Monarch, pushing an empty oil barge through Seymour Narrows. This is one of the few proper push rigs in British Columbia. The tug fits into a notch in the barge. They can operate in far more bad weather than a tug pushing on a ordinary barge. On the east coast of the United States there are some huge barge-tug combinations. They often have a deep notch so the tug is further protected by the barge.
The tug went through major changes for this job. Two 1,325 bhp. engines replaced the old engines. In addition to a high wheelhouse, the bow was rebuilt and strengthened.

River tug heading up the Columbia River. These tugs are designed for river towing only. They will take tows coming in from the sea via sea-going tugs and work them upriver for many miles. They take their tows through the locks in the dams.
When Seaspan arrives at Astoria with one of the big lime rock barges, a river tug will take over and push it to the cement plant.

Narrows, there is a lot of current. Unfortunately, it changes direction unexpectedly. Normally the tug comes in at a slow speed with her three barges strung out on the gear. When she gets close to the tieup, consisting of sticks strung out between buoys, she will try to determine which way the tide is running. She will slowly drift up to the sticks with the first scow shortened up to the stern. When she gets close enough to grab a standing wire, one of the crew will grab it with a pike pole. As soon as it is over the tow bitt, the bridles are let go and the tug manoeuvres clear of the scow before it gets jammed in between the scows in the tieup. The crew knocks the bridles off the link and the towline is slowly shortened up. When the next scow is shortened up, it is brought alongside another tieup. After getting a line to the sticks, the third scow is brought in and made fast. The crew then finish putting lines on the other scows. The scow lights are picked up and the tug heads over to the other side of the tieup to yard out her three empties.

It does not always go that easily. The current will change direction without notice, or the wind will gust the opposite way and the fun begins. It is not unusual to see the tail scow suddenly sail past the tug followed by the other scows. As soon as the towline comes tight, it starts to turn everything around. Tail scows have been known to head for the other side of the tieup. This wraps the towline round the anchor buoy and brings everything to a halt.

There have been many experiences in Duncan Bay. One of the boats with two loads came into the Bay. The skipper hung the first barge off, leaving the mate to finish the job. The mate was down on the sticks getting a jammed wire loose. As the boat approached the sticks with the second barge, the skipper was handling the boat from the after station while they heaved up the towline. The boat hit the sticks with a bang. The skipper looked around to see the mate in mid-air where the sticks had been a split second ago. They then had to try and retrieve the mate out of the water. He was able to get back on the sticks and finish tying up the scows.

When a tug is towing barges in passes and narrows where there is a lot of current, she must keep control of her tow as much as possible. If the tow gets in a back eddy when the tug is in the main current, the barge can take off in a different direction. This can cause damage and can, in some cases, sink the tug.

The Island Ranger, with two barges, was bucking a big tide between Fiddle Reef and Ten Mile Point without making any headway. It was decided to work into the back eddy off Jimmy Jones Island and attempt to use it to get to Ten Mile Point. The tail scow got into the back eddy first. It quickly passed the head scow, turned and hit the head scow hard enough to punch a hole in it. Fortunately, the hole was above the water line. As it was now in the same current as the rest of the tow, it headed back behind the head scow again. The tug slowed down when the gear came tight in order not to break the bridles. After things settled down, the tug bucked up the back eddy and within a few hours was around Ten Mile.

Other situations have not worked out as well. When there is too much of a southeast gale to get loaded chippers around Cape Mudge on the way to Duncan Bay, the tug will often go up through the Yaculta Rapids. Due to turns and currents in the rapids, you can only get through with two loads at slack water. A small tug is dispatched to take the third barge through the hole and give it back to the tug on the other side. The tug then takes the three barges southbound through Seymour Narrows on the next tide.

On one of these occasions, all went as planned until the tug with two chippers got to Little Dent Island at the western end of the Yacultas. It was the usual dark, rainy night with a lot of driftwood in the channel. The tug was a couple of minutes late on the tide. The tug slowed down as the current changed and the tail scow started to pass the rest of the tow. The head scow started to turn around by itself. The sudden jerk on the gear created by the scows wanting to go in opposite directions, broke the bridles on the head scow. Now loose, it headed back into the narrows by itself.

After getting clear of the narrows with the remaining scow, the tug handed it over to the small boat and headed back into the narrows. As the current runs around eight or nine knots with many whirlpools, the skipper expected to see the lost scow high and dry on an island or upside down after ripping her bottom out on a rock. Much to his surprise, the barge was sitting peacefully in the middle of a big whirlpool. The tug hooked on to it and waited till slack water to get out of there and get her other two barges from the small boat.

The speed of tug and barge has increased over the years. This is often a surprise to pleasure craft that have a bad habit of cutting in front of a tug. The type of tow makes some difference of course. A big rail barge towed by a modern tug will make far better time than a loaded log barge. An empty log barge or a big rail barge usually move faster than a lot of the passenger boats did in the forties.

INLAND AND STERNWHEEL TUGS

Barges were towed alongside by the sternwheelers on the inland lakes. They were usually handled alongside. In some areas further south, they towed astern with the towline made fast on the king post.

Of course, traditional tugs were used as well. They had a long housework and often no towing winches. On the lakes and rivers of the interior where heavy swell is not a problem, they do far more pushing and alongside towing than on the coast. The river push tugs are quite a different operation and, as with all river work, not without its share of thrills and spills.

6

SHORE TO SALVAGE

Seaspan has a shipyard and base all together in North Vancouver. Most large companies have a similar situation though it may be spread over a larger area. A small company may have its vessels at a rented space on a dock and its office uptown.

THE SHORE ESTABLISHMENT

We see the tugs passing with their tows and are unaware they are only part of the industry. Without the support of the office, supply, shipyards and repair personnel, the industry could not operate for one day. The duties of the staff working ashore will vary according to the company and its size. In smaller companies, one person may have responsibilities for various departments.

The size of the company can range from an owner-operator all the way to a large corporation. Regardless of size, the company depends on shore staff to keep it operating even if the company depends on shipyards, mechanics and accountants from other businesses.

In all companies, there is an upper management structure that is responsible for the overall business decisions, including operations of the tugs and barges. As many companies operate out of more than one port, the managers may not be in the same city as the tugs.

All successful companies depend on a hardworking sales staff. This will often involve not only securing new contracts, but solving the problems that may come up between customers and the company. Large companies may have separate divisions with their own staff, such as log barging.

When a customer notifies the company that he wants a product transported, a ship assisted, or a barge or boom towed, the company must start getting the correct type of equipment to the job on time. Even in more routine operations, such as towing chip scows, getting the right tug on the job at the right time requires a lot of jug-

gling. Things do not always go as planned. Weather plays a big factor in the industry. A tug and tow can get slowed down or held up for days. That a barge may not be loaded on time or a ship may not arrive as scheduled are but a few of the problems encountered.

Sorting all this out falls on dispatch. The dispatch department is always a busy place even when there is a slow down. When things are slow, any tugs that are not required are tied up and the crews sent home. The method of keeping track of all the tugs and floating equipment depends on the company and the type of towing it handles. Log towing companies that have to keep track of hundreds of booms in various storage grounds, often have a different system than a barge or a ship docking business. In some offices a large map is placed on the wall so the dispatchers can see where the tugs are.

Most companies have conference calls several times a day on the single side-band radio or through ship-to-shore phone. The tug will give her position and ETA. As well, the tug will receive any new orders. If the tug is operating within range of FM radio, dispatch will keep in constant contact with the tug.

There are always surprises and if the dispatcher is not familiar with the problems encountered at sea, there will be difficulties. An American tug bound for the Columbia River called dispatch to inform them that they were going to be late for their ETA at the bar. The dispatcher asked why. The skipper informed him that they had run into a southeast gale and twenty foot seas. The dispatcher asked what difference that made and they were expecting the tug to be on time. The skipper repeated the weather and sea conditions and the reduced speed. The dis-

Pacific Towing Services in Port Alberni is a branch office so the boats are tied up with other vessels and the office is in a building close by.

patcher still could not understand what the problem was and kept asking the tug. The tug must have had a problem with his radio as he did not answer all the rest of the calls! If dispatch is not familiar with a particular type of tow, it can ruin all the plans. A tug was heading northbound with a tow of logs when it got a call from dispatch to pick up a barge later in the day after his tow was tied up. The skipper said the time was fine but the day was wrong, as it would be another day before he would reach there with his slow-moving tow.

The tugs, at times, seem to have a problem with their electronic calculators or their scratch pads. Their ETA's have been known to be in error. Conditions, such as wind and current, can also play a part of inaccurate ETA's. This can create constant frustration and replanning.

The personnel department is another area where there is usually never a dull day. Not only must they work with union agreements and government regulations, they must be able to get the right crew aboard a tug often without too much notice. As arrival and departure dates for tugs are ever changing, arranging a crew change can be a major challenge.

The vessels must have supplies, such as food and parts. This responsibility falls on the purchasing department. When they get orders for items, they must get an ok from whatever department is responsible for them. They then must make sure the suppliers deliver the items on time.

Large companies will have a shore captain. His job is to make sure all the needs of the deck department are handled. This involves all gear, such as towlines and bridles. He usually is heavily involved with government regulations and operational safety. He will keep the deck officers informed of changes and company policy. He will often have to supervise an operation or make decisions as to the safety of a tieup.

In one form or another, all outfits whether big or small, will depend on the engineering staff to keep the boats and equipment operational. Small companies may employ outside staff for this. As a company gets bigger, it will have its own people. Many trades are needed to keep a modern tug working and, even with large companies, some outside experts are used.

In this day of electronics, they must have radar and radio repairmen on call day or night. A tug operates twenty-four hours a day and can not afford to wait for repairs. Large companies may have their own staff for this specialized work.

Safety is something that can not be ignored or workers' compensation rates will rise. Lawsuits can spell trouble as well if people are too careless. These points must be considered without making operations slow or too difficult. Large companies will have a safety department for this, but even the small company will have someone looking after these matters.

The tugs operate round the clock and so must the shore establishment. It is too expensive to have a tug and crew waiting for the office to open. The amount of problems that must be overcome on a daily basis can only be touched on in a book such as this.

MEMO to all marine personnel. - The new menus are as follows:
Breakfast - Watered down mush.
Lunch - 1 tuna fish sandwich.
Dinner - 1 TV dinner.
No mugups.

OTHER OPERATIONS

We have shown a few types of the jobs concerning tugs from British Columbia and Puget Sound. There are many others, such as the tugs involved in construction, fishing and tending dredges. Most areas where they boom logs have small tugs. Offshore towing goes on all the time. The American tugs do far more of this than the Canadian boats.

Every bit of construction along the waterfront involves tugs. Most companies have their own small boats.

Powerful U.S. tugs are involved with towing long distances on a steady basis to the north slope of Alaska, Hawaii and other parts of the world.

Canadian tugs certainty have done a lot of towing across the Pacific as well. Recently, the Seaspan Commodore towed new barges from Shanghai to British Columbia. The Sudburys became famous for towing WW11 Liberty Ships to Japan.

Tugs work as fireboats in some harbours. They often have powerful nozzles connected to large pumps. They can assist the regular fire departments with waterfront fires.

The ever changing fishing industry uses tugs for a number of jobs. This may range from towing fish camps to herring scows.

Getting a line on the Mills Trader in a North Pacific gale. This attempt was not successful but eventually a line was put aboard with a rocket gun.

SALVAGE

Salvage brings visions of Spanish treasure and fabulous wealth but, in the real world, salvage involves working with every day commercial vessels. This can be just as exciting and often includes getting into dangerous situations. There are two types of salvage in which the tugboat industry could be involved. These are rescue salvage and salvaging ships or cargo that have sunk or gone aground. At one time this was big business. Modern electronics and more modern ships have reduced the number of ships that get into trouble on the coast. There were tugs that specialized in this work. These vessels, such as the Salvage Chief and the 800 ton Salvage King, were equipped with salvage gear and decompression chambers as well as towing equipment. Divers were often part of the crew. The Sudbury 1 and 11 were salvage tugs, though they were engaged in coastal and foreign towing as well.

Today, salvage of sunken vessels is often a combined effort of derrick, tug and diving companies. All the different types of salvage work would fill a book by itself. If we get a big ship such as a large tanker aground, it will take the combined effort of the U.S. and Canada as well as the efforts of trained personnel from many companies.

Rescue salvage usually requires a larger tug to go out to a disabled ship. She must get her towline up on the ship and tow it to a designated port. This, as the weather is often bad, is difficult to accomplish. Before modern electronics, finding the ship could present a problem. The relatively small tug often had to fight North Pacific gales and huge seas in order to get the ship to a safe port. In one prominent salvage book, it mentions that rescue-salvage work is easy and does not present too many problems. They, obviously, did not try picking up a ship in a North Pacific gale.

The Island Sovereign's rescue of the 10,000 ton Maplecove, in 1952, was one of the more hair-raising examples of this type of salvage. After turning back due to 80 mph. winds and 40 foot waves, she eventually picked up her tow 55 miles west of Swiftsure lightship. This was done in 20 foot seas and gale force winds. Captain Art Warren got the ship to Vancouver. The Sudbury's rescue of the Makedonia in the North Pacific near the Kamchatka Peninsula in 1954, was considered "one of the great feats of the sea" by the Vancouver Province. The Agnes Foss rescued the Margo in 1953, and towed it to the Columbia River despite heavy weather. These are but a few of the many times tugs have pulled in disabled freighters.

Before the tug even gets near the ship a lot of things need to be done. The tug may be on another job when the call comes in. She must be relieved of her tow by another usually smaller tug. As a rule, she will have to take on bunkers and extra men and stores. The office will try to work out an agreement with the ship's agent as to the type of tow it will be. You do not risk tug and crew without having some form of agreement. In some cases, it will involve a straight towing agreement but if the job is at all doubtful as to its outcome, it will be done on a Lloyd's Standard Form of Salvage Agreement "no cure no pay" known as Lloyd's Open Form. As the amount paid often depends on the difficulties encountered as well as the success of the rescue, every detail from preparation to the delivery is recorded.

The ship will have given a position based on celestial navigation and dead reckoning. Sights are often hard to determine in the North Pacific due to days of cloud cover and low fog. Other vessels, such as coast guard ships, may find the ship first. Radio direction-finders are useful in locating the ship. With modern electronics and the use of aircraft this is not the problem it once was. The ship will be drifting in wind and current and the tug master must take this into account when setting his course for the rendezvous.

Upon arrival, the tug must get a heavy towline up to the ship and secure it. A light line is sent up first, usually with a line-throwing rocket or line-throwing gun. A heaving line can be used, but in heavy swells and strong winds it is hard to get close enough for this operation. If the tug bumps the ship in any part of the operation, damage will occur to the ship, the tug or both.

Rockets are required aboard ocean-going vessels over 500 tons. They are hard to aim. Rockets fired across the wind tend to head up into the wind, while rockets fired down wind will fly high. They have been known to come back to the tug which keeps the crew on its toes. The lines get wound round the housework and have to be cut loose. If rockets are used to get a line to a tanker, the rocket can cause the tanker to blow up. There goes the profit, especially on a "no cure no pay" agreement.

A line-throwing gun, developed after WW1, is more practical. A streamlined line-carrying projectile is fitted over the barrel of the gun. A blank cartridge propels the projectile. The line is a special non-fouling type. This line is usually nylon and today is coiled by the factory on a

special frame so it will not foul. On a calm day it has a range of 70 yards with a medium-sized line. The line and projectile are still affected by wind and the gyrations of the tug so it is still not an easy matter to get a line up to the ship.

After the light line is sent up, a heavier line called a messenger, which is heavy enough to be used on a windless without breaking, goes up next. This will be attached to the heavy towline. There may be an intermediate-sized line sent up between the rocket line and the heavy line. It is extremely important that no strain comes on these lines while this operation is taking place.

The towline is usually made fast to the ship's anchor cable (chain). Wire flattens and chafes where it goes through the fairlead. The ideal method is for the ship to bring one anchor inboard and disconnect it so the towline can be shackled to it. This often is impossible due to the sea conditions. The anchor can be secured on deck and the chain let go at the first shackle.

From this, it can be seen that the tug must be able to stay in position near the ship for some time while the crews of both vessels handle all this gear. The low after deck must not take too many seas aboard if the crew is going to be able to function. A ship will lie at a different angle to the wind depending on the location of her housework and she will be drifting down wind at a considerable speed. A ship with all her housework midships, such as a lot of WW11 ships, will lie broadside to the wind while a ship with all her housework aft will lie bow to the wind. Most tugs with their housework forward will lie with the bow down wind. The tug master must take all these things into consideration when positioning his tug to get a line aboard. He does not want a heavily laden ship drifting down on top of him or it could sink him. As with most towing operations, this crucial ability can only be gained by years of experience and not by reading books.

The job of getting the towline aboard is made even more difficult if there is no power on the ship. In 1967, the Sudbury 11 was sent to pick up an old Victory ship, the Millstrader. She had run out of fuel on her way across the Pacific with a cargo of teak. It turned out the chief engineer and the skipper had sold too much fuel before they departed.

The Sudbury 11 got some guidance from a military aircraft that had been sent out to locate it. When the Sudbury got there, it was blowing the usual gale. The Millstrader was a totally dead ship. The Chinese crew had taken to busting up the little wooden furniture to burn for heating and cooking. The captain and the chief were English but the rest of the officers were Chinese.

The crew on the tug contacted the ship's crew using morse code on a signal lamp. The mate on the ship knew what to do but, without power, it was going to be impossible to connect the towline to the anchor cable. It also was going to be hard and slow to even get the towline up on the ship's deck. The first attempts were made to get a heaving line up to the heaving ship. This had to be abandoned as the wind and seas were increasing. After several tries, a line was fired up to the ship with a line-throwing gun.

Then the long job of getting the towline up began. The mate on the ship got his crew working hard to successfully pull up larger-diameter lines until the heavy towline

The Sudbury II, last salvage job. The barge, Koko Head, hit a rock and rolled over. The cargo was salvaged. The barge was eventually righted and towed to Vancouver.

Tanker off Victoria after being towed in from sea.

could be pulled up on deck. This required excellent sea-manship on the part of the ship's mate and his crew. The tug had to stay in position while this long procedure took place which involved very difficult boat handling by the skipper. The crew on the tug had to work all the gear, despite the fact the after deck of the tug was frequently swept by waves.

Eventually a bridle was made fast to the ship's bitts. Towing in open ocean on a soft wire was difficult. After the tow got underway, it was discovered the ship had a leak and there was no way of pumping it out. The Sudbury 11 headed for the top end of Vancouver Island to get some shelter. By the time they got out of the weather off Port Hardy, the ship had a significant list. The tug was able to get alongside and put her salvage pumps to work. The ship was then towed to Vancouver where the cargo was discharged along with the skipper and chief.

An even worse problem occurred when the tanker, Mandoil 11, and the freighter, Suwahara Maru, collided well off the Washington coast. There was a fire on the tanker taking 11 lives of a 43-man crew. She started losing cargo. The Sudbury 11 got a line on her 180 miles off the coast. The line parted in bad weather. The tanker had lost an estimated 500,000 gallons from her 10,000,000 gallon cargo, putting her bow awash. Eventually, the wreck was towed stern-first by the Sudbury 11 and the Island Sovereign. The Island Monarch hooked on to the bow to steer her. They eventually anchored in Nootka Sound.

Meanwhile, the cargo vessel was towed to Victoria after a hectic voyage by the Arthur Foss. The ship was unloaded in Victoria.

Even modern ships run into trouble at times. In March, 1995 the 32,611 dwt. bulk carrier, M.V. Wave, broke her tail shaft 720 miles west of the Queen Charlotte Islands. The Seaspan Commodore picked her up in storm force winds and towed her to Vancouver. The tow took ten days through winter gales and heavy seas

The next type of salvage encountered on the west coast is refloating stranded ships. They often break up very quickly after coming ashore. Nevertheless, there have been some extraordinary examples of this type of salvage, such as the salvage of the Yorkmar, near Grays Harbor in 1952, by Fred Devine's, Salvage Chief. He was able to anchor his vessel and, after several attempts, get a towline on the stricken ship. This had to be repeated after the anchors dragged on the Salvage Chief. On the next attempt he got the ship off the beach by pulling on his anchors, pulling with his engines and having the large "Red Stack" tug, Sea

Lion, pull on her bow. This was considered an amazing feat.

The salvage of the Greek freighter, Glafkos, off the west coast of Vancouver Island by the Sudbury was another of this type of salvage work as was the barge, Forest Prince, by the Sudbury 11. Vessels stranded on inside waters had a better chance of being pulled off than ships that hit the rocky outer coast.

In some areas, beaching gear can be used to give an extra pull. When beaching gear is used, heavy salvage anchors are dropped by the salvage vessel. Heavy lines are run out to the stranded ship. Large tackles are laid out on the deck of the salvage vessel. When the pull starts, the tackles are heaved up on winches. They do not work too well on the outer coast of Vancouver Island but have been successfully used on the Washington coast.

The next type of salvage is recovery of the cargo and, in some cases, the machinery of the stricken ship. There have been many successful operations and not a few failures. Most of the older wrecks that occurred in relatively shallow water had at least part of the cargo and machinery salvaged. In later years, salvagers picked up most of the brass that had not been taken originally.

There have been several examples of salvaging the cargo despite the odds. One of these was the Alaska bound Koko Head. This large barge was being towed from Puget Sound to Alaska loaded with containers on deck and machinery and supplies in the hold. The barge hit a rock in Hiekish Narrows, took on water and rolled over. Some of the containers, the hatch and a few other bits and pieces headed for the bottom. The Sudbury 11 towed the upside-down barge to Khutze Inlet and anchored it. Repairs were made to the crumpled bow. Divers then had the dangerous job of cutting the chains that held the containers. The diver would not know what to expect when he cut a chain; some containers floated, some sank. The containers were lifted by derricks on barges that had been brought in for the job and loaded on waiting U.S. barges.

Unlike most barges, this one had a big hold. Fortunately, the hatch that had been lost when the barge turned over had been found and recovered by the divers. The hatch cover was put in place and secured. In order to get at the cargo, a hole was cut in the bottom of the upside-down barge. A new diesel engine and lighting plant were recovered. The engineering staff immediately washed out the engine and shortly had it running. This prevented rust and deterioration taking place. When the cargo had been removed, the hatch was welded in place and the hole repaired.

After a few tries, and a sinking, the barge was righted and towed to Vancouver. This took months of work, many tugs, a log barge, scows and lots of supplies. For a time, there were 48 men on the Sudbury 11. The Pacific Challenge, an ex-whaler, had been brought in for the job. Aircraft were constantly bringing in supplies and personnel.

Ships, such as the 650 GT. SS British Columbia, in 1917, have been lifted from the bottom, as have many smaller tugs, barges and fishing vessels. This usually involves the use of heavy-lift equipment or floats as well as tugs. Wooden barges usually broke up even under the best conditions before they could be salvaged.

Picking up a sunken vessel at New Westminster. Most salvage work is not that glamorous. The author spent an afternoon diving and rigging a herring skiff and a crane in the middle of a boat show. The only annoying thing about that job was the amount of oil that collected around his mouth.

Before any salvage begins on grounded ships, a salvage master must be appointed. A survey of the situation must be done including the cargo and the bottom. In most cases, the salvage master is a specialist in salvage. He may bring other experts with him. Salvage is a very complex and often dicey business. He must have more than an average knowledge of naval architecture, rigging, diving and seamanship. After surveying the ship, he will draw up a written salvage plan. This often has to be approved by other interested parties, such as the underwriters. He then must bring in all the men, equipment and supplies. As these jobs never go as planned, he must be able to have "plans B and C" ready to go. This is, at best, an expensive operation so time is against him.

Most of these jobs could not be done without divers. At one time this was all done with "hard hat" (standard gear). In some situations heavy gear has an advantage over SCUBA. The diver is solid on the bottom (if what he is standing on does not collapse) so he can better handle tools. He has better communication with the surface which is an asset when working with heavy-lift gear. Communication is absolutely necessary for welding and a lot of cutting. A lighter form of surface-supply gear is still used for any serious jobs. There is a lot of equipment available today to aid the diver.

Damaged vessels often have to be patched before any salvage attempts can be made. This is very seldom an easy job. There were standard patches developed in the war that would be fitted to the outside of the ship. These would not work if there was a rock through the bottom of the ship. Pontoons, in the form of other vessels, were often used to float a ship into a beach for patching. Smaller vessels are often lifted with derricks for transport to a shipyard.

There are so many ways to approach salvage work, of any kind, that many books have been written on the subject. But you can be sure, most jobs will present difficulties you will not find in any book.

Good sailing

Did you hear that tug's ETA?

APPENDIX

GLOSSARY

There are many terms used in the towboat industry that are not used in other seagoing activities. Some are used locally and some pertain to a type of towing. A few of these are listed below.

Alongside- Tow made up to the tug or two vessels made fast side by side.

Athwartships- Anything at right angles to the fore and aft line of the vessel.

Backing and filling- Tug going ahead and astern to turn the tug in a small space. Tugs often do not have much room to manoeuvre in so they go ahead and astern. The rudder must be shifted for each direction.

Backing line- Line running forward from the tug to the barge.

Bridle- Wire or chain forming a Y shape for towing barges or ships.

Dogs- A metal object connected to a wire that is driven into a log so it will not come out of a boom. There are several types of them. Some are screwed into the log.

Hawser (U.S.)- Towline.

Light tug- Tug running without a tow.

Make up to a barge (U.S.)- The barge is put alongside the tug with spring line, head line and stern line. Usually done for making a landing.

On the hip- Tug fast alongside barge, make up to or pick up.

Pendant or pennant- A short length of wire used for connecting barges together when towing. They are part of the towing gear on a log tow. They connect to the towline.

Pick up barge (Can.)- The barge is put alongside the tug with spring line, head line and stern line. Usually done for making a landing.

Pigtail (U.S.)- Chain pendant.

Skeg- Fixed rudders at the stern of a barge. They are often set at an angle and are shaped.

Spring line- Line running either fore or aft to keep a vessel from shifting. On a tug, a line running aft to take the forward thrust.

Stern line- Line from the after bitts on the tug.

Stern pins- Pins at the stern to restrict the movement of the towline. They keep the towline from going around the stern at sea. They keep the towline from going under the counter when handling a tow in a harbour. They are sometimes called norman pins.

Swifter- Usually a log pulled over a boom so the boom will keep its shape. Wire swifters are used in open water. Dogs are used to hold the logs in.

Tandem- More than one barge or more than one tug on a tow.

Yarding- Sometimes called juggling in the U.S. Moving booms or barges around in order to make up a tow. This can involve shifting booms or barges that cover the items the tug wants.

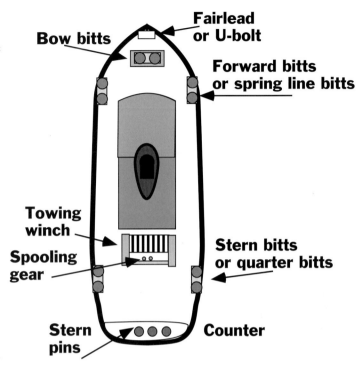

TUG TYPES

There are many variations of each type of tug. A conventional tug can either be single screw or twin screw. It can have Kort nozzles or open propellers (wheels). The nozzles can be fixed with rudders behind them or steering nozzles (nozzle turns but not the propeller).

The tractor tugs can use cycloidal propulsion. They have vertical adjustable blades. Power can be supplied in any direction by adjusting the angle of the blades.

Steerable rudder propellers are used on other tractor tugs. The nozzle and the propeller can rotate 360°. Two of these units are used side by side. If they are located forward of the center of the tug it is a tractor tug. If they are located aft they are a reverse-tractor tug.

Variable pitch propellers can be used on conventional tugs or tractor tugs.

Some conventional tugs use bow thrusters. This can be a cheaper way of making them handier.

The hull shape will be determined by the type of work the vessel is designed for, government regulations and the opinions of the owner. Each type of tug is more useful for one type of work than another. As an example, nozzle boats have a far greater pulling power on heavy loads but are not as good with lighter, faster tows such as rail barges. The pulling power is rated by bollard pull.

BIBLIOGRAPHY

4,000 Years - Sooke Region Museum -1990.

A Manual of Marine Engineering - Charles Griffin & Co. - 1904 - A. E. Seaton.

American Merchant Seaman's Manual - Cornell Maritime Press Inc. -1964 - F. Cornell & A. Hoffman.

American Practical Navigator (Bowditch) - U.S. Navy Hydrographic Office - 1966

Basic Seamanship and Navigation - McGraw-Hill Book Company - 1951 -Edmund A Gibson.

Chambers Navigation - W&R Chambers Ltd. -1910? - John Don-W.J. Caird.

First Growth - B.C.F.P.

Glory Days of Logging - Superior Publishing - Bonanza Books - Ralph W. Andrews.

Hansen Handbook - Lowman & Hanford Co. - 1931 - Raymond F. Farwell.

How Wooden Ships Are Built - W.W. Norton & Co. -1918 origional - H. Cole Estp. -Reprint.

Marine Engineering - Scranton International Textbook Co.-1894-1900.

Modern Seamanship - D. Van Nostrand Company -1903 - Austin M. Knight.

Modern Towing - Cornell Maritime Press -1994 - John Blank.

Nautical Surveying - D. Van Nostrand - William Jeffers - 1871.

Navigation and Nautical Astronomy - United States Naval Institute -1943 - B. Dutton.

Nicholls's Seamanship & Nat. Knowledge - Brown, Son & Ferguson Ltd. - 1938 - Charles H. Brown.

Pacific Steamboats - Superior Publishing Co. -1958 - Gordon Newell &Joe Williamson.

Pacific Tugboats - Bonanza Books - G. Newell & J. Williamson.

Practical Marine Engineering - Marine Engineering Inc -1901 - William Durand.

Reeds Seamanship - Thomas Reed & Company -1880 - 1925 - Sunderland.

Shipbuilding in Iron and Steel Vol 2 - William Collins, Sons, & Co. Ltd. - 1880? - Samuel J.P. Thearle.

Steel Ships - Charles Griffin & Co. - 1944 -Thomas Walton -J. Baird.

The Chartmakers - NC Press Ltd. - 1983 - Stanley Fillmore-R.W.

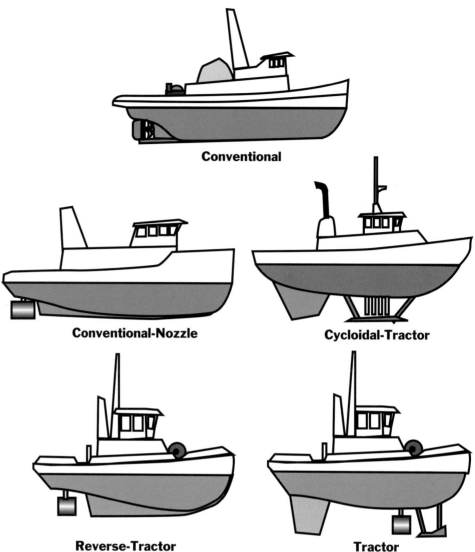

Conventional

Conventional-Nozzle

Cycloidal-Tractor

Reverse-Tractor

Tractor

Sandilands.

The Marine Power Plant - McGraw-Hill Book Company -1942 - Lawrence B Chapman.

The Marine Steam Engine - Longmans Green & Co. -1918 - Richard Sennett - First 1882.

The Oxford Companion to Ships & The Sea - Oxford University Press - 1976 - Peter Kemp.

The Sea Chart - David & Charles:Newton Abbot -1973 - Derek Howse-Michael Sanderson.

The Shipwrights Trade - Conway Maritime Press/Cornell Maritime Pr. - Orig 1948 reprint 1981 - Sir Westcott Abell - Reprint.

Theoretical Naval Architecture Vol I & II - William Collins, Sons, & Co. Ltd. -1878? - Samuel J.P. Thearle.

Tugs, Towboats and Towing - Cornell Maritime Press - 1967 - Edward Brady.

U.S. Coast Pilot - Alaska to Beaufort Sea - U.S. Dept. of Commerce - 1964.Wire Rope Hand Book & Catalogue - British Ropes Canadian Factory -1955.

Sawlogs on Steel Rails -1997 - George M McKnight.

The Lighthouse - McCelland and Stewart Ltd. -1975 - Dudley Witney.

The Journal of Navigation - The Royal Institute of Navigation -1974 - Vol. 27 No. 4

Towboats to the Orient -1970 -R. S. Mansfield & W. L. Worden.

Westcoast Mariner

Wooden Ship Building - Rudder Publishing Co. -1919 - Charles Desmond.

Wooden Boat and Ship Building - Frederick J. Drake & Co. -1941 - Richard M. Van Gaasbeek.

Working in the Woods - Harbour Publishing - Ken Drushka.

Wrinkles in Practical Navigation -1937 22 ed. - S.T.S. Lecky - 1st ed 1881.

INDEX

Let's put it this way cap! You have 2 hours 23 minutes and 35 seconds to get to a fuel dock and I would not bother putting it astern when you get there.

Other Books by Western Isles

SMOKE ASH and STEAM

R.Sheret
102pp 81/2x11 PB 115 illus.118 photo.
ISBN 0-921107-04-8
$24.00

The steamship opened commerce on the West Coast of North America. While there have been a number of publications on the ships, this long overdue book for the first time talks about the development of the engines. The engines are from coastal and river boats and some deep water ships from the 1830s to 1960s including paddlewheel steamers.

This old technology is explained simply for anyone interested in marine history. We are pleased to say steam enthusiasts overseas have been enjoying this book.

DIVERS' SEAMANSHIP & NAUTICAL KNOWLEDGE

R.Sheret
126pp 7x81/2 ISBN 0-921107-02-1
$16.95
While written for recreational divers, this book explores methods of returning to a dive site or wreck and of rigging lifts. Charter boat operators would benefit from the weather and current information and man overboard recovery. The section on ship construction, identification of findings and some history would aid wreck researchers and divers.

For other marine books handled by Western Isles send for free catalogue to:

WESTERN ISLES
2962 Leigh Rd., Victoria, B.C.
V9B 4G3
Canada

westisle@islandnet.com

ABOUT THE AUTHOR

R.E.Sheret has 40 years experience on coastal vessels, fourteen years as mate and nineteen as master. He has photographed many subjects including tugs and ships. He started diving in 1954 and later was trained in salvage diving. He is now a member of the Underwater Archaeological Society of B.C. This, along with his interest in historical marine events on the west coast of British Columbia, has prompted his third title depicting the history and work life of a west coast tug and the booms and barges it has towed from inception to the present time. Tugs Booms & Barges is an interesting read for general audiences.